Praise for *Can You Say...*

W9-BVK-267

"Joan Detz is the Emily Post of speech communication. She tells you what's right, what's wrong, what works, what doesn't work. You don't have to wing it anymore."
  —James F. Fox, past president, Public Relations Society of America

"Joan Detz's book *Can You Say a Few Words?* is imaginative, practical, and necessary. All of us who are asked to speak can learn a great deal from it. Keep it close by."
  —Stephen D. Harlan, vice chairman, KPMG Peat Marwick

"*Can You Say a Few Words?* by Joan Detz has helped me to speak better. I recommend this book to anyone who wishes to use words well."
  —Norman Vincent Peale, author of *The Power of Positive Thinking*

"Once again, Joan Detz has packed her new book with helpful tips for the novice as well as the experienced presenter."
  —Hans Decker, vice chairman, Siemens Corporation

"A very helpful, very practical book."
  —Rabbi Harold S. Kushner, author of
    When Bad Things Happen to Good People

"If you need to present yourself or your organization to the public, you need the skills offered by Joan Detz."
  —Raymond W. Goodnoe, president,
    Bucks County Association of Township Officials

"Joan Detz is the sharpshooter of speechwriting and speech-giving. Her books are the silver bullets that help hit the target every time!"
  —Betty Serian, deputy secretary for safety administration,
    Pennsylvania Department of Transportation

"Joan unearths the science of speechwriting and delivery in a way everyone can understand."
  —Gene Rose, president,
    National Association of Government Communicators

Praise for *It's Not What You Say, It's How You Say It*

"I see a lot of books on public speaking. This one I'll keep."
    —Terrence McCann, executive director, Toastmasters International

"If you want to make a big investment in your business career, buy this little book by Joan Detz."
    —Joe Gonzalez, president,
      New Jersey Business and Industry Association

"Hers is the best practical advice available on the subject of public presentations."
    —Jack Boyd, assistant to the president and chief of staff,
      The College of William and Mary

"Her book helps alleviate speakers' anxieties so they can concentrate on their message."
    —Loren Gary, editor, *Harvard Management Update*

"Fresh advice . . . keen insights. A pithy manual . . . an excellent tool."
    —*Publishers Weekly*

"No one has better advice and more creative ideas than Joan Detz."
    —A. W. "Bill" Dahlberg, chairman and CEO, Southern Company

Praise for *How to Write & Give a Speech*

"A how-to classic."
    —*The Washington Post*

"In international business, knowing how to speak efficiently and effectively is the key to success. This handy book will help busy executives master this important skill."
    —Dr. Mitsuru Misawa, president,
      Industrial Bank of Japan Leasing (USA)

"Joan Detz has gone a long way toward taking the mystery out of writing and giving an effective speech. For this, I will find it hard to forgive her."
    —Former Governor Mario Cuomo

CAN YOU SAY A FEW WORDS?

11./6

808.5
Detz

Also by Joan Detz

How to Write & Give a Speech
It's Not What You Say, It's How You Say It
You Mean I Have to Stand Up and Say Something?

CAN YOU SAY A FEW WORDS?

How to Prepare and Deliver a Speech
for Any Special Occasion

JOAN DETZ

St. Martin's Griffin
New York

CAN YOU SAY A FEW WORDS? Copyright © 2006 by Joan Detz. All rights reserved. Printed in the United States of America. No part of this book may be used or reproduced in any manner whatsoever without written permission except in the case of brief quotations embodied in critical articles or reviews. For information, address St. Martin's Press, 175 Fifth Avenue, New York, N.Y. 10010.

www.stmartins.com

Library of Congress Cataloging-in-Publication Data

Detz, John.
    Can you say a few words? : how to prepare and deliver a speech for any special occasion / Joan Detz.—1st ed.
        p. cm.
    Includes bibliographical references and index.
    ISBN 0-312-35352-9
    EAN 978-0-312-35352-0
    1. Public speaking. I. Title.

PN4129.15.D48 2006
808.5'1—dc22

                                                                2005044684

First Edition: April 2006

10   9   8   7   6   5   4   3   2   1

In memory of my mother and father,
who taught me to speak up

CONTENTS

Special Occasions

Resources

ACKNOWLEDGMENTS

So many people have helped in so many ways. I would particularly like to thank these individuals, who made the whole process go smoother:

Carole Alfano, New Hamphire State Senate
Paul Burgess, the White House
Dominic Chianese, *The Sopranos*
Mike Field, Johns Hopkins University
Leigh Glenn, National Automobile Dealers Association
Tim Hayes, freelance corporate writer
John Knotts Jr., Lackland AFB
Karen Leniart, U.S. Customs and Border Protection
Ted McCleskey, USAF Pentagon
Brian Melton, RadioShack Corporation
Dawn Rodeschin, U.S. Army, Ft. Leavenworth
Dan Sieger, Toyota Motor Manufacturing North America
Lucinda Trew, Duke Energy
Steve Vanderplas, U.S. Coast Guard
Sandy Williams, NASA
Bill Woodbridge, Naval Sea Operations

I am grateful to Dennis Anniballi and Dyon Anniballi, who shared their computer expertise so generously . . . and to the reference librarians at Bucks County (Pennsylvania) Library, who tracked down research details with tenacity and patience. Our nation's public libraries are a public treasure, and a portion of this book's proceeds will be used to support them.

Special acknowledgments go to Scott Donaldson (The College of William and Mary) and Gordon Symonds (Millersville University). Many years ago, they taught me the value of a clean sentence. I remain grateful.

And, finally, my greatest appreciation goes to my son, Seth Rubinstein. His cooperation made this book possible. And his indefatigable spirit always inspired me to make it better.

CAN YOU SAY
A FEW WORDS?

INTRODUCTION

The ability to give a "special occasion" speech has always been important. But, it has never been more important than *now*.

I originally wrote this book back in 1991. Since then, so many historic events have touched our lives . . . and we have seen how powerful, inspirational speeches can help us "honor the moment" (whether a moment of joy, tribute, mourning, dedication, or accomplishment).

Certainly, no event has riveted us more than 9/11. It was immediately followed by an unprecedented need to give thousands of eulogies. But, in time, it was followed by something else: a growing wish to honor *all* the landmark moments of our lives . . . to acknowledge special events in our communities, our careers, and our families . . . to take these fleeting passages, and somehow make them *last* with our words.

We know this:

Words make a difference. Words focus our attention. Words honor the moment. And in doing so, they heal . . . they prod . . . they inspire.

That's the purpose of this new edition: to help you mark the events of your own life . . . so you can "say a few words" that are as special as the occasion itself.

It might start out simply enough:

- Your company wants to give you a service award, and you'll have to say a few words at the ceremony.

- Your alma mater calls and asks you to say a few words at the centennial alumni dinner.

- A senior executive dies, and you're expected to say a few words at the memorial service.

- Your team wins the state championship, and your principal asks you to say a few words at the victory banquet.

- Your parents celebrate their 50th anniversary, and you'll want to say a few words at their party.

Well, that's the big question: Can you?

Can you "say a few words" that will capture the audience's attention, keep their interest, and further your cause? What's more, can you prepare under deadline pressure?

All too often, the answer is no.

The sad truth is, most people would rather do *anything* than stand up and say a few words. And the emotional stress that often goes hand in hand with these special occasions makes your job even harder.

I know. For two decades, I've been writing speeches and coaching executives at top organizations across America. And I've seen accomplished speakers turn to mush when they had to make an emotional retirement speech. I've seen confident administrators lose control when they had to offer a eulogy. I've seen tough CEOs stammer when they had to face a TV interview.

Special occasions *demand* special speeches. And sorry is the speaker who doesn't live up to the audience's demands.

One man, a highly competent executive, told me, "It's funny. I've faced angry shareholders; I've given lots of financial presentations. But when I had to pay a farewell tribute to a colleague . . . well, that was the toughest speaking assignment I ever got. I wanted to come up with something really special to suit the occasion, but I just didn't know where to begin."

And he's not alone. I've heard similar stories from speakers in all walks of life.

I lecture on speechwriting throughout the country—to Fortune 500 corporations, professional organizations, colleges, all sorts of groups. Invariably, someone in my seminar will say, "I've got a problem. I have to introduce my boss at a big conference, and I don't know how to start. What makes a good introduction? Can you give me some pointers?"

Yes, I can. And that's exactly what I'm going to do in this book.

I've written my book in sections, organized alphabetically by occasion. So if you're in a hurry—and who isn't?—you can turn straight to the relevant chapter: awards, building dedications, eulogies, Q&A sessions, retirement tributes, toasts, whatever.

You'll get quick advice, podium-tested examples, and practical tips that will help you "say a few words" for *any* special occasion.

And at the end you'll find a preparation checklist, a glossary of rhetorical techniques, and an annotated bibliography (describing books and Web sites where you can get terrific quotations and anecdotes).

The advice in this book has proven helpful to my clients over the years. I hope it proves helpful to you—so the next time someone asks you to "say a few words," you'll be able to mark the moment with a speech that's as special as the occasion.

All the best!

SPECIAL OCCASIONS

ANNIVERSARIES

Be ruled by time, the wisest counselor of all.

Plutarch

Suppose the principal at your local high school completes 20 years of service, and your town wants to host an anniversary tribute. Or your company wants to celebrate 50 years in business. Or your nature club wants to garner attention for 10 years of environmental accomplishments.

How can you come up with a speech that's as special as the occasion? Here are 12 ideas for an anniversary speech people will remember long after your event is over:

1. Say Why the Anniversary Is So Important

When Kraft Foods marked the 100th anniversary of Jell-O, the occasion brought together dignitaries, employees, and media—and hailed the country's largest-selling prepared dessert as an American cultural institution.

2. Turn Back the Clock

People love to reminisce, to go back in time, to remember the way things used to be. So turn back the clock 20 years, 50 years, 5 years—whatever.

What were the hit TV shows? Who made front-page headlines? What captivated the blogs?

In short, what were people talking about when this person got started? Use these details to grab your audience's attention.

For example, you could say:

Back in 1985, something called a compact disc appeared on the market . . . four-wheel-drive vehicles hit our roads . . . and the phrase "ozone layer" entered our national vocabulary. And a new science teacher by the name of Jane Smith came to Penn High School. Today, on her service anniversary, we've gathered to salute her dedication to our school.

3. Return to the Scene

In 2002, on the 10th anniversary of the race riots that devastated Los Angeles, President George W. Bush went to the scene, speaking in a church hall near the riot area.

4. Recognize Changes That Have Occurred Over the Years

What's different now? Have the passing years brought big changes? If so, point them out. Cite specific improvements. Give details. Share examples. Create a vivid understanding in the mind of the audience.

5. Cite the Good Qualities That Have Remained Constant Over the Years

Has the person kept a sense of courage, of curiosity, of fairness? Has the company honored its founding principles—even during tough times?

   If so, cite those qualities, and remind the audience of their current value.

6. Articulate the Shared Emotions

After the 1994 bombing of the Alfred P. Murrah Federal Building in Oklahoma City, President William Clinton gave a stirring address at the memorial service. No president could have done a better job rallying the nation's spirits at that difficult time.

In 2004, when formal ceremonies were held to mark the 10th anniversary, private citizen Bill Clinton returned, offering this perspective: "Oklahoma City changed us all. It broke our hearts and lifted our spirits and brought us together."

7. Articulate Your Beliefs

What better time than an anniversary to restate your philosophy?

When President Lyndon Johnson marked the 10th anniversary of the Government Employees Incentive Awards Act at Constitution Hall in Philadelphia, he used the ceremony to restate his beliefs: "I believe in the tight fist and the open mind—a tight fist with money and an open mind to the needs of America."

8. Use an Inspirational Quotation or a Bit of Local Color

When the University of Pennsylvania celebrated its 250th anniversary, President Sheldon Hackney tapped into the university's origins as a "charity school" established by Ben Franklin.

Quoting an inspirational line from a 1749 Franklin pamphlet, President Hackney said, "The great aim and end of all learning is to be able to serve others. That is why our university exists. That is why all universities should exist."

9. State the Abiding Lessons

Anniversaries come . . . and go. But their lessons can be timeless.

Back in 1974, when President Gerald Ford addressed the 75th

annual convention of the Veterans of Foreign Wars, he placed war (and peace) in this perspective: "All of us who served in one war or another know very well that all wars are the glory and the agony of the young."

10. Share Your Enthusiasm

On the 30th anniversary of *Apollo 17*'s moon mission, David King (then deputy director, NASA Marshall Space Flight Center) personalized his greeting:

> I've been looking forward to this day with childlike excitement. With us today are some of the heroes who had a huge impact on what I wanted to do with my life. . . .
>
> You don't have to raise your hand, but how many of you remember—as a child—standing in your backyard at night looking up at the moon . . . in the hopes of seeing one of the astronauts walking around up there?
>
> The fascination with humans going to the moon kept me in hot water with my mother. Many times she would have to tell me to go to bed: "Quit watching that show about space." Today, she understands.

11. Honor the Sacrifice

Lt. Gen. Bruce Carlson offered these remarks at the Prisoner of War Recognition Ceremony on the 61st anniversary of the Bataan death march:

> Every person who has worn the uniform and fought in battle understands the nature of sacrifice. But as a people united in freedom, we owe special respect and gratitude for those who were captured. They suffered tremendously at the hands of their captors—virtually all of them subjected to physical torture and incredibly harsh conditions. Yet they maintained their faith in their

Nation, and they nurtured the hope that one day they would re turn home. . . .

America must never forget their courage.

12. Say It with Something Other Than Words

Don't feel you have to rely on words alone. Anniversary ceremonies can be enriched by:

- *Silence*. When world leaders gathered to honor the 75th anniversary of the Battle of Gallipoli, Australian and British warships fired their guns, and everyone observed one minute of silence.

- *Applause*. When a popular retiree returned to a company's anniversary event, no words seemed adequate to express the goodwill in the air. So the audience simply rose and applauded with great enthusiasm.

- *Song*. When a coach celebrated his 5th winning season, his team honored him with a rousing rendition of the school song.

AWARDS: GIVING THEM AND GETTING THEM

Honour is purchased by the deeds we do.
Christopher Marlowe

Did one of your employees submit a prize-winning suggestion? Did a member of your speakers bureau earn a service citation? Did a teacher on your staff get national recognition?

When you present an award on these special occasions, you'll want to give a speech that's equally special—a speech filled with praise, admiration, and respect for the honoree.

Of course, you'll also want to give a speech when you're the recipient of an award—an acceptance speech filled with gratitude, appreciation, and respect for the group that's honoring you.

GIVING AN AWARD

When someone does something good, applaud! You will make two people happy.

Samuel Goldwyn

Here are eight ideas that can help you give an award speech that's more personal, more inspirational, and more memorable:

1. Express Your Admiration for the Honoree(s)

When President Harry S. Truman presented the congressional Medal of Honor to fourteen members of the Navy and Marine

Corps after World War II, he expressed his abiding respect for the recipients this way:

> We are not a warlike nation. We do not go to war for gain or for territory; we go to war for principles, and we produce young men like these. I think I told every one of them that I would rather have that medal, the congressional Medal of Honor, than to be president of the United States.

2. Talk About How You Know the Honoree

Have you worked on the same programs? Did you join the company at the same time? Do you live in the same neighborhood, go to the same church, or do volunteer work for the same causes?

If so, make that connection clear to the audience. They'll appreciate the personal ties.

A caution: If you *don't* know the person who's getting the award, don't pretend. Audiences are quick to spot a phony connection.

Instead, say something simple and sincere: "I've heard many fine things about Paul, and I'm pleased to meet him tonight. The plant foreman told me about Paul's heroic efforts, and it's an honor to present him with our company's humanitarian award."

3. Cite the High Caliber of Previous Recipients

Who won the award last year? Five years ago? A decade ago? Cite their distinguished reputations—and express gratitude to be included in such respected company.

4. Paint the Big Picture

Let's suppose you're honoring an employee for a suggestion that will save the company *x* dollars each year. Why not multiply that figure by the total number of employees to show the great potential of these money-saving suggestions?

5. Praise the Dedication

Did your recipient drive through a blizzard to meet her obligations? Work on weekends to complete his project? Postpone her vacation to provide a crucial service?

Cite that sacrifice. Offer generous praise. Extraordinary contributions deserve extraordinary award speeches.

6. Create a Sense of Urgency

When I conduct speechwriting workshops, I'm often asked for ways to "spice up" an award ceremony. As one workshop participant put it, "Since our utility hands out service awards every year, the program gets stale after a while."

You can make an award ceremony seem fresh by giving it a sense of immediacy.

Show what's happening at the very minute you present the award. For example: "We have gathered here tonight to honor our volunteers. In the two hours we are meeting, x number of people will call our hotline to ask for help."

7. Use Interesting Statistics

Statistics don't have to be boring. Listen to the vivid statistics that Dr. David Snediker, vice president of Battelle, used when he spoke at an awards reception in Ohio:

> In 1965, a mechanic could fix any car on the road if he or she understood 5,000 pages of service manuals. But today, that mechanic has to be able to comprehend 465,000 pages. That's the equivalent of 250 Columbus telephone books!

8. Cite Qualities That Make the Recipient Uniquely Valued

Be specific. Give real-life examples. Tell a flattering anecdote about the person. Show what makes this person special.

GETTING AN AWARD

> *Publishers and literary agents once told me I could never*
> *make a success at writing about Chinese people. I thought of*
> *that the day I stood before the King of Sweden to receive the*
> *Nobel Prize.*
>
> *Pearl S. Buck*

Accepting an award is a great honor—exciting, prestigious, and touching. But it can also be a little bit scary. Scary because the audience has such high expectations. How can you ever meet them?

Well, you could always follow in the footsteps of Yogi Berra, who once began an acceptance speech by saying, "I want to thank all the people who made this night necessary."

But if that's not your style, maybe you'll find some inspiration in the following approaches.

Express Affection for the Organization

When Oprah Winfrey received a 50th anniversary medal from the National Book Foundation, she expressed her affection for authors:

> More than movie stars and rock stars and famous politicians and world leaders, I love authors. I love authors because in the beginning was the word.

When Jimmy Stewart was honored by the Film Society of Lincoln Center in New York City, he responded with great affection:

"I ask God to bless all of you, and when he takes our lives to his editing room, I pray he will be as kind to each of you as you've been to me tonight."

Share Your Award with Those Who Deserve Credit

When Jack Welch was given the Private Sector New Englander of the Year Award, he graciously accepted the honor on behalf of the 25,000 employees who made GE successful.

Acknowledge the Support of Your Family

If your family has been a source of inspiration, say so.

When singer Tracy Chapman received a Grammy Award, she expressed these personal thank-yous: "To my mother, who bought me my first guitar, and to my sister, who is my best critic, my best audience, and my best friend."

Acknowledge the Importance of Your Hometown

In 2005, Len Roberts, CEO of RadioShack Corporation, was honored with the Brotherhood/Sisterhood Citation from the National Conference for Community and Justice. He cited his family's affection for the community of Ft. Worth:

> We are all proud to call Ft. Worth home . . . it's our family's nerve center. It's a great city. . . . In fact, the nonprofit group, Partners for Livable Communities, named it one of the most livable cities in the nation!
>
> What's that bumper sticker say? "I wasn't born in Texas, but I got here as fast as I could."
>
> That's me. My job brought me here . . . but it's by choice *now* that I stay.

Express Your Humility

When Rev. Billy Graham was offered a star on Hollywood Boulevard back in the fifties, he turned down the honor.

About 30 years later, he reconsidered and became the 1,900th star on that sidewalk. But he kept his humility, reminding stargazers, "We should put our eyes on *the* star, which is the Lord."

Honor Your Colleagues

When actress Barbara Stanwyck received an honorary Oscar, she held it up and spoke of her late costar William Holden: "He always wished that I would get an Oscar; and so, tonight, my Golden Boy, you've got our wish."

Recognize Your Competitors

Did you win a state basketball championship? Walk away with the top sales award for your company? Score a much-talked-about victory?

Praise your competitors for their ability, their hard work, their sportsmanship.

Let Your Personality Shine Through

When Bette Davis was honored by the Film Society of Lincoln Center, she received a standing ovation that lasted more than a minute and a half. After acknowledging the cheering crowd, the actress looked right at those 2,700 Davis fans and gave them a bit of the acid wit they had come to love over the years.

"What a dump!" she said, bringing down the house with her well-timed delivery of that classic Davis line.

Try Candor

At age 79, Mary Roebling, the first woman to head a major bank, retired as chairperson of the National State Bank. And in her mid-eighties, she found herself busier than ever.

Within just one week, she participated in three award ceremonies. She was named USO Woman of the Year, she presented an award to honor Professional Women in Construction and Allied Industries, and she was saluted by the Daughters of the American Revolution in Trenton, New Jersey.

Ms. Roebling's response? "I keep thinking people are confusing me with someone else."

Share an Anecdote

When she accepted an award in 2004 from the Philadelphia chapter of the Public Relations Society of America, Debbie Albert of ARAMARK told this story about her work:

> Let me share with you a typical call for a public relations person at ARAMARK. I had a phone call the other day from the ARAMARK manager at the Baltimore Zoo where ARAMARK provides food and retail services.
>
> It turns out that Paris Hilton was at the zoo shooting an episode of *The Simple Life*. Our manager there told me that we had provided Ms. Hilton with a shirt to wear and that the shirt said ARAMARK on the front.
>
> "You mean Paris Hilton has the word 'ARAMARK' emblazoned across her chest?" I shouted. "Go see and let me know."
>
> So I held the line while he checked out Paris's chest. He reported back, *thankfully*, that no, the name of the company was *not* on her shirt.
>
> Crisis averted.
>
> This is what we deal with every day, right?

A Little Humor Can Work Wonders

When British Prime Minister Margaret Thatcher was honored at The College of William and Mary in Williamsburg, Virginia, she made a lighthearted reference to the Colonies' 18th century separation from England:

> But let me hasten to add that all is forgiven; no hard feelings; you've done such a wonderful job. May I add, if there had been a woman prime minister at Downing Street at the time, it would have been handled so very much better.

When Robin Williams accepted the Cecil B. DeMille Award for lifetime achievement at the Golden Globe Awards in 2005, he used humor to put everything in perspective:

> I want to thank you for having Prince, William Shatner, Puff Daddy, and Mick Jagger on the same stage. That is a sign of the apocalypse.

George Burns knew the value of humor when he received an honorary degree from the University of Hartford at age 92. Burns said, "I can't wait to run home and tell my mother about this. She always wanted me to be a doctor."

Keep It Brief

At 98, Jack Horwitz was honored by the Long Island Medical Center for his role as one of the hospital's founders. Many speakers praised him, but Mr. Horwitz kept his remarks disarmingly brief: "It's nice to hear everything you said while I'm still alive. I'm glad I'm here. I think I said enough." And so his speech was finished.

When I think of all the audiences who have suffered through long, boring, pompous acceptance speeches, it makes Mr. Horwitz's sincerity and brevity seem all the more noteworthy.

IF YOU'VE LOST

Lose a prestigious award? A big account? An important game? Try to put your loss in perspective.

Yes, you have to acknowledge defeat . . . but no, you don't have to dwell on it. Say you did your best, but acknowledge that the winner did better.

Above all, be a gracious loser. Don't be mean-spirited. Let the victors enjoy their moment in the sun.

When Preacher Roe was with the Brooklyn Dodgers back in the forties and fifties he had a favorite saying: "Some days you eat the bear. Some days the bear eats you. Yesterday, the bear ate us."

CHOOSING THE AWARD

Lenox, Inc. (the maker of fine china and crystal) created the gifts that were presented to President George W. Bush at his 2005 inaugural luncheon: exquisite crystal hurricane lamps. This gift was especially appropriate because Lenox has created fine china for the White House for more than 80 years.

You probably don't have the budget to commission one-of-a-kind cut crystal. But you do have other options.

Plaque? Trophy? Paperweight? Engraved tray? Monogrammed desk set? The choices are almost endless.

Unfortunately, so are the pitfalls. Before you pick any award, ask a few practical questions. Use this checklist:

_____ *Is it too big to fit into a recipient's briefcase or luggage?* A loving cup might prove awkward for your honoree to carry onto an airplane.

_____ *Is it too fragile to survive a long trip?*

_____ *Is it perishable?* A manager was honored at an out-of-state conference. Unfortunately, she was presented with a basket of regional foods, which spoiled before she got home.

_____ *Will it just collect dust?* A gigantic paperweight might only take up desk space. Something more functional (say, a radio, or a desk set) could be used every day.

_____ *Is it appropriate?* For example, why give a gold watch if you know the recipient already wears a special watch? Maybe a fine pen would be more appropriate.

_____ *Will your cost-cutting measures result in a cheap-looking award?* Every award ceremony has budget limitations. But no matter what your spending cap, make sure your award still looks top of the line. Opt for a small bowl of great quality, rather than a large bowl of mediocre quality.

If you're having the award engraved, consider where you place the inscription. For example, if MAN OF THE YEAR appears on the front of a standing desk calendar, only the honoree will see it. If you place that inscription on the opposite side, all the visitors who sit across the desk from him will see it.

BIRTHDAYS

Birthday: The funeral of the former year.
Alexander Pope

Whether announced or not, birthdays have a way of becoming public knowledge.

If your staff throws a coffee-and-cake birthday party for your secretary, or if your father decides to throw himself a 75th bash, or if your boss deserves a few special words on her 50th birthday, could you say something appropriate?

These ideas might help:

WISHING SOMEONE A HAPPY BIRTHDAY

"When They Were Your Age . . ."

Mention interesting achievements of famous people at certain ages. (Note: The annotated bibliography on page 155 describes useful reference books and Web sites that will help you find clever details.)

For example:

- Age 43: John F. Kennedy becomes the youngest American president.

- Age 68: Architect Frank Lloyd Wright takes two hours to quickly sketch a house called Fallingwater . . . and his client, pleased, says, "Don't change a thing."

- Age 75: Alexander Graham Bell invents the telephone.

Here's how you can work these bits of trivia into a birthday tribute: "We're all here to wish our manager a happy 50th birthday. Of course, we're wondering what surprises he has in store for us this year. After all, Henry Ford was 50 when he introduced some crazy idea called 'the assembly line.' And Henry Kissinger was 50 when he won the Nobel Peace Prize.

"Now, we don't know exactly what *our* manager is cooking up for his 50th year, but we hope it's something good, and we wish him the very best."

Use a Catchy Quotation

Turn to a good reference book or Web site and find a lively quote. Maybe . . .

- T. S. Eliot: "The years between fifty and seventy are the hardest. You are always being asked to do things, and yet you are not decrepit enough to turn them down."
- Lord Grey (at age 75): "I am getting to an age when I can only enjoy the last sport left. It is called hunting for your spectacles."
- Bernard Baruch: "To me, old age is always fifteen years older than I am."

Talk About the Year the Person Was Born

Was your honoree born in 1970? What were the big events of the year? What was the number-one bestseller? Who made the top news stories?

This historical trivia will capture the audience's interest—and show the honoree that you cared enough to prepare a clever speech.

Go Beyond Words

Sometimes the best birthday tributes don't use words. Consider these creative approaches:

- When George Delacorte, the philanthropist and founder of Dell Publishing Company, turned 97, the New York City Parks Department wanted to salute him for the wonderful things he had given to the city's parks over the years. Their special tribute? A rendition of "Happy Birthday to You" played on the animated animal clock that bears his name at the Central Park Zoo.

- When Elizabeth, the Queen Mother, turned 90, plans for a military parade were scrapped in favor of a less traditional parade—a parade that would include an Aberdeen Angus bull, six chickens, and a pack of dachshunds. Why the animals? They represented some of the 300 organizations of which the Queen Mother was a patron, including the Poultry Club, the Dachshund Club, and the Agricultural Society of Scotland.

CELEBRATING YOUR OWN BIRTHDAY

> *I'm 53 years old and six feet four. I've had three wives, five children, and three grandchildren. I love good whiskey. I still don't understand women, and I don't think there is any man who does.*
>
> *John Wayne*

Can't imagine what you'd say if someone threw a big birthday bash in your honor?

Here's how some people approached their birthdays:

Play a Mathematical Game with Your Age

James Thurber once said, "I'm 65, and I guess that puts me in with the geriatrics, but if there were 15 months in every year, I'd only be 48." Alas, Thurber was better at comedy than math: If a year had 15 months, he'd have been 52. But still, you get the idea.

Express Satisfaction with Your Family

Lord Lytton once said, "At 60, a man learns how to value home." You could build on a quotation like that to express the joy you receive from having a wonderful family, the satisfaction you take from relaxing in your own home, the pleasure you get from working in your garden.

Acknowledge the Advancing Years

Not so young as you used to be? No one is. But, consider Rose Kennedy's spunky comment on her 100th birthday: "I'm like very old wine—they don't bring me out very often, but I'm well preserved."

Try a Little Humor

For example, I once gave this quip to a client to use at his 50th birthday party:

"Gore Vidal once said, 'For certain people, after 50, litigation takes the place of sex.' Well, I hate to disappoint all the lawyers in this town, but . . ."

Poke Fun at Your Image

When Prince Charles turned 40, he sported a LIFE BEGINS AT 40 button and poked fun at his image as an eccentric. The prince gave a carefully crafted speech that mocked his tabloid image as a kooky person who talks to plants:

> Only the other day I was inquiring of an entire bed of old-fashioned roses, who were forced to listen to my demented ramblings on the meaning of the universe as I sat cross-legged in the lotus position. . . .

His self-parody brought cheers from the 1,500 youths who were invited to celebrate the prince's birthday.

Find Advantages in Growing Older

Perhaps something like this:

> Jean Renoir, the French film director, once said, "The advantage of being 80 years old is that one has had many people to love." Well, that's true. And, when I look around and see all of you at this party, I'm grateful for the family and the friends that *I've* been able to enjoy these 80 years. I love you all. And I thank you for giving me such a happy birthday."

Tap the Wisdom of Your Years

Pearl Buck made these comments in her 80th year:

> Would I wish to be "young" again? No, for I have learned too much to wish to lose it. . . . I am a far more valuable person today than I was 50 years ago, or 40 years ago, or 30, 20, or even 10. I have learned so much since I was 70. I believe I can honestly say that I have learned more in the last 10 years than I learned in any previous decade.

If You're Caught by Surprise . . .

You're working in your office, you hear a little commotion outside your door, you look up—and all your cronies have gathered to surprise you with a birthday cake.

Might as well join their spirit of fun and respond with something funny. A manager I know got a surprise from her staff when they serenaded her with a birthday cake blazing with 50 candles. Her good-spirited response? "Well, getting older may not be so great, but it sure beats the alternative. Thanks for thinking of me!"

No one expects you to give a real speech under these circumstances. A smile and a simple lighthearted response will carry the day.

Final Reflection on Birthdays

> *I never feel age. If you have creative work, you don't have age or time.*
>
> Louise Nevelson

CHANGE OF COMMAND AND NEW JOB PROMOTIONS

I have climbed to the top of the greasy pole!
Benjamin Disraeli,
upon being named prime minister

Change of Command speeches do more than announce a new leader. And job promotion ceremonies do more than announce someone's new title. These presentations accomplish three important goals: They salute one person's accomplishments . . . inspire others to achieve peak performance . . . and set a positive tone that defines the entire organization.

Here are some successful techniques:

Cite Credentials

This is no time to be modest. This is also no time to be general. Promotion speeches need to cite impressive credentials—and the best way to do that is by offering specific details.

Here is how Under Secretary of Defense E. C. "Pete" Aldridge Jr. spoke at the promotion ceremony of Col. Michael L. Bruhn:

Mike graduated in the top 5 percent of his West Point class of 1982. His degree was in nuclear engineering. He also holds a master's in the same subject from Berkeley. As we all know, we are in the midst of a transformation of our national defenses into a more technocentric force. Anyone who questions Mike's ability to thrive in this brave new world should consider the title of his master's thesis: 'Thermal Effects on the Divertors of TOKOMAK During Plasma Disruptions.' Mike is definitely the right man for the times. . . .

A reading of his performance evaluations holds no surprises for me. They are peppered with such descriptions as versatile; totally dedicated; exceptional technical expertise; invaluable; first choice; right stuff; beyond his years; tremendous talent; dynamic; top-notch; sets the standard.

I'll stop before we all start feeling inadequate. Mike, your service to this nation and all she stands for has been without peer. . . .

There are many worthy callings to be answered. But in a free nation amidst a dangerous world, there is no higher calling than the profession of arms. For in a free nation, it is the profession of arms that makes all the other callings possible. . . .

Congratulations, Mike. . . . And now let's get these eagles pinned on.

Describe the Significance of the New Position

In 2005, at Lackland Air Force Base, Maj. Gen. Paul Lebras spoke at the promotion ceremony of Col. Jacqueline (Jacky) S. Walsh. He put her accomplishment in perspective with these words:

I want to tell you what a significant achievement it is to make colonel in the U.S. Air Force. Fifty-plus years of statistics tell us that only one out of every ten officers who is commissioned makes it to colonel. Obviously, some separate from the service after their initial commitment, but for those who remain, it gets more and more competitive. Making colonel means you are in the top 6 percent of the officer corps. It is to colonels that we entrust command of our groups and wings—putting them in charge of thousands of men and women. So promotion to colonel represents not just a great personal achievement, but an incredible vote of confidence from the Air Force.

Place Your New Position in an Industry-wide Context

Ruth Shaw became the first female president of Duke Power Company, one of the nation's largest electric utilities. In her first presidential speech to the annual meeting of U.S. Women in Nuclear (Chicago, 2004), Ruth Shaw used her new role to focus attention on women in the electric utility industry:

> I'm reminded of the way the original "woman in nuclear," Madame Marie Curie, was once described: "An overachiever who cooked, cleaned, discovered radium, won a couple of Nobel Prizes, and raised a Nobel Prize-winning daughter, but who never forgot how to make a good pirogi" . . .
>
> I was invited to talk with you today not because I'm a nuclear engineer or physicist. I am privileged to stand at the helm of Duke Power Company, which operates seven of the country's finest nuclear units . . . I'm a woman who *leads* women in nuclear, *values* women in nuclear, and is working hard to make sure we tap your talents wisely.

Acknowledge Your Family's Contributions

Here is how Lt. Col. Carol Northrup honored her family during her 2004 pinning ceremony at Barksdale AFB in Louisiana:

> Having my parents here today means a lot to me. They have always been supportive of my goals . . . even when I announced (at the ripe old age of 10) that I wanted to go to the Air Force Academy!
>
> My father is a retired school superintendent. He is also a Marine. (There's no such thing as a "former" Marine, you know.) He was my hero growing up, and for as long as I can remember, I've tried to follow his example. He taught me that school is important, and girls *can* be good at math. He taught me how to break in my combat boots, and that no one likes to hear excuses. He taught me

that I can be whatever I want to be . . . if I'm willing to work hard enough. And he taught me there is almost nothing that ails you that can't be fixed with a little exercise!

My mother was a public school teacher for nearly 40 years, and she's the strongest person I know. She taught me the importance of my faith and that I can be a good officer *and* a good mom. She taught me how to iron a shirt, how to pack for a move, and that being kind is not a sign of weakness. She also taught me: family *always* matters . . . and whatever exercise won't fix, a nap probably will!

By their constant example, my parents taught me the Air Force core values of integrity, service, and excellence long before I took the oath. For that—and for so much more—thank you.

Consider a Memento

The words you say are important. But props, gifts and mementos can make their own powerful statements.

On his desk in the Oval Office, President Kennedy displayed a plaque with these words: "O God, thy sea is so great, and my boat is so small." The plaque was given to him by Adm. Hyman Rickover, founder of the modern nuclear Navy. Admiral Rickover made a tradition of giving a plaque with these words to the commanding officer of each new Polaris submarine.

CHILDREN AND SCHOOL GROUPS

Children are unpredictable. You never know what inconsistency they're going to catch you in next.

Franklin Jones

You're a businessperson, and you'll be speaking to teens at career night. You're a police officer, and you'll be visiting area schools to discuss drug abuse. You're a parent, and you'll be talking to Girl Scouts about a big community project.

How can you get your message across to *kids*?

Involve the Children

Author Andrea Warren received the 2004 William Allen White Award for her children's book *Surviving Hitler: A Boy in the Nazi Death Camps*. Over 55,000 Kansas school children voted to select this as their favorite book for grades four to six.

In accepting the award, Andrea Warren spoke directly to the students in the audience. Notice how she hooked the children immediately by asking questions, encouraging them to raise their hands, and using the word "you" to get them involved.

Do you like Halloween? Most of us like dressing up and scaring each other and going through haunted houses. We scream and we laugh. How many of you like scary stories—movies and books? Yes, most of you. We put ourselves into those stories. We become the hero as we imagine ourselves clinging to a log in a raging river, or running away from the bad guys, or rescuing a baby in a burning house.

We like these stories because we get a vicarious thrill from them. That means we experience the event and the feelings without actually having to be there. Nightmares can work the same way. They give us a way to work through something scary. Afterwards we can wake up in our own bed, or leave the movie theater and go outside and breathe fresh air, or close the book and then sit down to dinner. The bad images start to fade away. We smile and we say, "Whew! That isn't me. I'm still okay. I guess my problems aren't so bad."

Of course, sometimes real life *is* scary, and we can't wake up from it.

It can be little things that happen. The alarm doesn't go off and you're late for school. . . . You forget your lines in a school play even though you had them memorized. . . . A classmate makes fun of you, or trips you in the cafeteria and you drop your tray and everyone laughs. . . .

Or it can be big things. Maybe you have trouble understanding your school work or paying attention in class and your parents have you tested and you learn your brain doesn't work right and you think it's your fault.

You're abused by the people who supposedly love you most, and you think it's your fault.

Your parents get divorced and one of them moves out and you think it's your fault.

You get kidnapped, and even though you know don't why, you're sure it's your fault.

Think about that last one. The bad guys now have you and you don't know what to do. Where are your parents? They're supposed to protect you.

Adults *are* supposed to protect children. But sometimes they can't. They may be far away and not know where you are. Or perhaps they've died. You have to take care of yourself. It isn't fair,

but there it is. Once you've accepted the unfairness, now what?
You have to become the hero of your own scary story. . . .

Use Language That Kids Can Understand

Be direct. Tell the kids what you're going to say . . . say it . . . and
then tell the kids what you told them. Don't pussyfoot around
the subject. Don't mince words. Children appreciate honest,
straightforward language—and respect the adults who give it to
them.

Use Props

Kids like things they can see, touch, taste, smell, and hear for
themselves. So bring along some props to grab their attention.
    For example:

- A woman who lectures on wildlife takes an injured owl into
  classrooms to show the impact of pesticides.
- An elementary school principal gives red ribbons to students
  to wear as a symbol of unity against the illegal use of drugs.
- A wellness center gives demonstrations of yoga and tai chi to
  encourage children in a wider variety of fitness options.
- A park ranger who talks about environmental issues takes
  "mystery boxes" into classrooms. Blindfolded kids put their
  hands into the these boxes and try to identify the objects
  they're feeling—perhaps seed pods, moss, wheat, a dandelion
  stem.
- Frenchtown, New Jersey, held a Fall Orange Festival—using
  color to attract attention and provide a consistent theme.
  What better way to capture attention for their first children's
  art show than to support it with orange-decorated store win-
  dows, orange food, and a juried orange pet show?

Be Approachable

Using a lectern might be fine in a large auditorium, but in a small classroom, it will just create an unnecessary barrier between you and the students.

In fact, if you're talking with small children, you might prefer to sit. Talking at their level will make you seem less intimidating and more approachable. You might want to have the children sit in a circle so everyone has a good line of sight and feels included.

Vary Your Pace

Kids get restless easily, and they're not the least bit embarrassed to show their boredom. So plan a variety of examples, demonstrations, and explanations. If your first effort fails, at least you've got a backup.

Include Everyone

Back to school night at Lenape Middle School, in Doylestown, Pennsylvania, effectively used American Sign Language to accompany the principal's speech.

Other options?

- Address students who speak English as a second language in their native tongue. No, you don't have to be perfectly fluent to do this. Just give them a simple greeting in Spanish or Korean or any other language that will make them feel included.

- Incorporate art. Several weeks before your appearance, ask students to provide illustrations for your topic. Have these drawings on display when the children enter the auditorium.

- Invite musicians, singers, and dancers. Every school has children who are especially talented in the performing arts. Let them play instrumental pieces or sing folk songs or perform dances that relate to your topic. Examples: patriotic marching tunes at a Memorial Day event, or Irish dancing for a St. Patrick's Day celebration. (A word of caution: Let the children shape their own event . . . please. Resist any temptation to let adults "do it better." I once attended an elementary school graduation that featured various musical offerings—all performed by adults. Apparently, the person who arranged this graduation ceremony thought adults would "do it better" than children. That might well be the case, but it would have been far more motivational to let children perform at a children's event.)

Allow Plenty of Time for Questions

Chances are, your listeners will have a host of questions and comments. If you overplan your presentation, you'll deprive them of the opportunity to take part.

Treat Kids with Respect and Kindness

As one first grader once told me, "I may be little, but I'm a person, too." And right she was.

Listen to children's comments with respect. Don't be bossy; it will just turn kids off.

Be friendly and caring. It was John Ruskin who observed, "Give a little love to a child and you get a great deal back."

Do Not Patronize

If you talk down to kids, they'll spot it . . . and resent it. Heed the wisdom of that wonderful children's author Maurice Sendak, who observed, "You cannot write for children . . . they're much too complicated. You can only write books that are of interest to them."

The same goes for presentations. You cannot "give a speech for children." You can only give speeches that are "of interest" to them.

COMMENCEMENTS

Kids in the first grade will be looking up to you, so watch what you say or do.

Reba McEntire,
at a Tennessee grade school commencement

You answer the phone and it's the alumni director from your alma mater, asking you to speak at the next commencement ceremony.

You're flattered, of course. It's quite an honor; probably the most prestigious speaking invitation you'll ever get.

You're excited, too. Thousands of students, parents, professors, administrators, reporters—probably the biggest audience you'll ever face.

And, truth be told, you're also a little nervous. After all, commencement speeches don't come along every day. So even if you're an experienced speaker, you probably haven't had an opportunity to give a commencement address. And that alone can create anxiety.

Well, relax. This is a perfectly normal reaction. Just take everything step by step, and you'll have one of the most satisfying speaking experiences of your career.

BEFORE YOU DO ANYTHING

Before you pick a topic, before you do any research, before you write one word of your speech, ask some basic questions about the commencement ceremony.

This list of questions will give you a better understanding of your role at the graduation event:

1. *Will there be any other speakers?* Most ceremonies feature one major commencement address; others feature several short speeches. If you're one of several speakers, ask to speak first, before the audience becomes fidgety. Find out what the other speakers will discuss, so you can avoid overlap.

2. *How long should I speak?* Use the university's guidelines, but take them with the proverbial grain of salt. If they've asked you to speak for 20 minutes, disregard their suggestion. That's too long. Instead, prepare a lively ten-minute speech, and you'll be a hit. Whatever you do, *don't* run on too long.

3. *Who will introduce me?* Send that person a completely written introduction—not a bio or a résumé, but a smoothly written introduction that's specifically tailored to your commencement address. You can learn how to do this in the Introducing Speakers chapter (see page 82).

4. *Will the ceremony have any special highlights?* Honorary degrees? Academic awards? Posthumous presentations? You might want to incorporate these details into your theme.

5. *What's unique about this commencement?* Is this the first commencement for the new college president? The last ceremony before a popular dean retires? The largest graduating class?

   Following the 9/11 tragedy, commencement at New York University changed in several ways. In previous years, a student would have sung the national anthem, but at the first post-9/11 graduation ceremony, the distinction of singing "The Star-Spangled Banner" was given to a New York City police officer. And, in another first, a Fire Department color guard was chosen to lead the formal academic procession.

6. *Are there any related activities I'll be asked to attend?* Commencement speakers are often honored at special luncheons, cocktail

parties, and receptions. Find out the timetable so you can make appropriate travel plans.

CREATING A MEMORABLE SPEECH

A commencement is a big event, filled with fine achievements and noble aspirations and grand emotions. Your speech must match the occasion.

Take the high road. Make your audience *feel* good. Give them something to remember with affection and with pride. Use these ideas for inspiration:

Give Your Commencement Speech a Strong Title

Titles offer advantages:

1. They appear in the graduation program.
2. They signal the tone of your speech.
3. They focus attention on your key theme.
4. They are often quoted by the press.
5. They sound a whole lot better than something listed as "graduation remarks."

Here are some good examples:

- Castles and Cobwebs (Norman R. Augustine, then CEO of Martin Marietta Corporation, giving the commencement speech at Embry-Riddle Aeronautical University)
- Choose Carefully: The Leaves of Life Keep Falling (former Chief Justice of the U.S. Supreme Court William H. Rehnquist, delivering the commencement address at Catholic University School of Law)

Share Your Personal Connection to the Institution

John P. Surma Jr., president and COO of U.S. Steel Corporation, used this opening when he gave the commencement address at Katz Business School, at the University of Pittsburgh, in 2004:

> I am honored to be asked to share some thoughts with you today, and I promise to be brief. I know that to succeed in business, you've got to move fast, and we might as well practice what we preach.
>
> Just a bit about myself and my connections to the University of Pittsburgh. As a native of this town, I grew up in the shadow of Pitt. My late father studied here, my wife earned her master's degree in public health here, I have a niece currently attending classes here, as well. My cousin Anthony Deardo is even a senior professor of metallurgy at Pitt. I'm constantly reminded that he's the *smart* metals guy in the family.

Salute the Parents

Parents put a lot of thought and care and—lest we forget?—*money* into their kids' education.

Salute their efforts. *Profusely*.

Praise the College

Desmond Tutu, as Anglican archbishop of South Africa, praised Wesleyan University for supporting black liberation in his country. In particular, he praised Wesleyan for backing economic sanctions against South Africa's racist, minority government.

Clarify Your Opinions

In her role as assistant to the president for National Security Affairs, Condoleezza Rice gave the 2004 commencement address at

Michigan State University. She began on a personal note and then moved into public policy:

> It is wonderful to be here in East Lansing. The academic in me is pleased to be at a university like MSU, respected around the world. The football and basketball fan in me is thrilled to be at the home of the Spartans. . . .
>
> I grew up in Birmingham, Alabama, before the civil rights movement—a place that was once described, with no exaggeration, as the most thoroughly segregated city in the country.
>
> I know what it means to hold dreams and aspirations when half of your neighbors think of you as incapable of, or uninterested in, anything higher. In my professional life, I have listened with disbelief as some explained why Russians would never embrace freedom . . . that military dictatorship would always be a way of life in Latin America . . . that Asian values were incompatible with democracy . . . and that tyranny, corruption, and one-party rule would always dominate the African continent.

Signify the Accomplishment

The Defense Language Institute is the world's largest foreign language school—teaching 85 percent of the U.S. government's foreign language classes. At the Arabic language graduation ceremony in 2005, Lt. Gen. William S. Wallace cited the importance of the graduates' accomplishments:

> This is a day you have anticipated for 18 months . . . maybe longer.
>
> You have no doubt worked very hard to become proficient in a difficult foreign language—one that most Americans either do not have the propensity or the commitment to learn. In fact, among the university students who begin studying Arabic, only 25 percent reach the third-year level. . . .
>
> You have accomplished a great deal in a relatively short

time. . . . College students who major in a foreign language study that language for four years—sometimes longer. And, their proficiency at the end of those years is typically *nowhere near* your current proficiency.

But I want to emphasize that your language abilities—while very important—are not the only skills your future commanders will value. Your knowledge about Middle Eastern cultures in particular—and your cultural sensitivity in general—will be especially useful.

Encourage Students to Make Bold Changes

Victor Kiam, chairman of Remington Electronics, Inc., speaking at Bryant College:

> What you are, our country will be. You have an absolutely idealistic opportunity to change the world for the better.

Use Some Humor

After thousands of hours of study (and many thousands of dollars of tuition), commencement audiences will welcome humor.

- At Brown University, comedian Bill Cosby reminded the graduation class, "Commencement means to go forth. And 'forth' is not 'home.'"

- When Colin Powell gave the commencement address at Howard University, he quipped: "Polls have been taken that show that 10 years after the event, 80% of all graduating students don't have a *clue* who their commencement speaker was. Well, you ain't gonna do that to *me*. The name is Powell. P-O-W-E-L-L."

Stress Human Relationships

Barbara Bush, giving the speech of a lifetime, at Wellesley College:

> At the end of your life, you will never regret not having passed one more test, [not] winning one more verdict, or not closing one more deal. You *will* regret time not spent with a husband, a child, a friend, or a parent.

Well said—and well received.

Honor the Values the Students Learned from Their Parents

At a basic military training graduation ceremony at Lackland AFB in Texas, Dr. James G. Roche (Secretary of the U.S. Air Force) included these remarks to the parents:

> To the parents, friends, and family here today, I know your hearts swell with pride as well.
>
> Some of you have worn the uniform of the United States Armed Forces. You know what it represents. And you know what basic military training is like.
>
> All of you, I'm sure, lost sleep the night after your son or daughter left for Lackland. Well, take a good, long look at your sons and daughters now, standing tall in this formation. They are very impressive, aren't they?
>
> They are strong—physically, mentally, and spiritually.
>
> They have learned the value of being part of a team and to commit to something larger than themselves.
>
> They arrived here because of the values you instilled in them. They endured this test because of what you taught them. But they succeeded on their own because of what these men and women before you have inside of them.
>
> As a parent, I know how proud you are of them.

Highlight the Career Opportunities

Charley Smith, as 2004 chairman of the National Automobile Dealers Association, spoke to Dealers Academy graduates and reminded them of the importance of new car sales in the United States:

> It's a one-trillion-dollar-a-year business—the largest retail business in the country.
>
> About twenty percent of all retail sales are generated at dealerships around the country. That's one out of every five retail dollars spent.
>
> We provide more than 1.1 million jobs. That's more than Chrysler, Ford, and General Motors combined.

Encourage Graduates to Remain True to Themselves

When my alma mater, Millersville University in Pennsylvania, asked me to return to campus to give the commencement address, I encouraged students to be proud of their unique talents:

> Remember who you are. And don't pretend to be anyone else.
>
> There was an eighteenth-century rabbi by the name of Zusha. A very wise man. And Rabbi Zusha used to say, "If they ask me in the next world, 'Why were you not Moses?' . . . I will know the answer to that question. But if they ask me, 'Why were you not Zusha?' . . . then I will have nothing to say."
>
> So remember who *you* are. And don't pretend to be anyone else.

I then cited Barbara Bush and Lady Bird Johnson, who earned our nation's affection and respect by remaining true to their own values.

DOES THE COLLEGE HAVE A UNIQUE STUDENT BODY?

Is the college all-female, or does it have an international mix, or is the graduating class composed of nontraditional students? Then speak about the characteristics that make these students special achievers.

For example, when former New York Governor Mario Cuomo spoke at the State University of New York at Stony Brook, he discussed racial and ethnic conflict in New York, and then suggested that the diversity of the Stony Brook student body might provide a lesson:

> This is a community that draws students not just from Long Island, but from France, Poland, China, Italy, Israel, Peru, and Vietnam. You're showing all of us how we can live together by learning more about one another.

TROUBLESHOOTING

Okay. You've analyzed the audience. You've prepared a fine speech. You've practiced for weeks. Nothing can go wrong, right?

Well, not exactly. Lots of little things can go wrong at a commencement. If you're not able to deal with them, they might prove unsettling.

And sometimes (I hate to tell you) even *big* things can go wrong. When former Mayor Ed Koch gave a commencement speech at the Polytechnic Institute of New York, fire broke out. As the school band broke into a stirring rendition of "New York, New York"—accompanied by the screech of fire sirens—about three thousand people, including many in flowing academic robes, had to file out of the building through thickening smoke.

Of course, most commencement pitfalls aren't so dramatic.

But you should still try to prevent as many glitches as possible. Scan this list of common pitfalls.

Problems with Caps and Gowns

We've all heard of commencement speakers who, en route to the lectern, stepped on the hems of their gowns and unceremoniously tripped. Or speakers who, in the middle of a dramatic gesture, felt their hats slip off.

All sorts of cap-and-gown horror stories can be prevented by providing the college with proper measurements, by arriving early to dress, and by carrying some safety pins and hairpins, just in case.

Problems with Microphones

Find out who's in charge of the sound system, and *get friendly with that person*. Ask, cajole, or even tip that person to stay nearby as you deliver your speech. Seriously.

Problems with the Media

Reporters may try to buttonhole you for an interview before the ceremony. Don't allow this to happen. You need to concentrate on your speech, and you don't want to be distracted by an interview.

Look reporters firmly in the eye and say, "I'll be happy to answer any of your questions—after the ceremony."

Of course, they may persist. They may tell you they're on a tight deadline, they may tell you they'll only ask a couple of questions, they may tell you they'll only take a few minutes.

Do not be moved. Stand firm. Say you'll be glad to meet with them *afterward*, and then turn away.

Remember, your top priority is to give a terrific speech for the thousands of people who have come to this commencement with great expectations. You simply cannot allow yourself to be distracted in those precious prespeech moments by one aggressive reporter who wants an interview.

Problems with the Weather

Outdoor ceremonies are nice—until dark clouds begin to form.

When heavy rain fell at a Columbia University commencement, President Michael Sovern suggested that the degrees be conferred all at once, just to speed things up. His suggestion was met with loud boos by graduates, who wanted to receive their degrees in the traditional fashion. So, Dr. Sovern capitulated and agreed, "All right, let's do it the regular way." However, when Dr. Sovern decided to cut his speech short, the wet crowd heartily approved.

Lesson: Be prepared to offer a shortened version of your speech if storm clouds dictate.

A FINAL CAUTION

Gowns are hot. Folding chairs are uncomfortable. Sound systems can be poor. Ventilation can be nonexistent. Under these less-than-desirable circumstances, don't be a commencement speaker who gives a long, boring speech.

If you can't give the world's most fascinating speech, at least you can give a short one.

Albert Einstein was not known for being a stimulating speaker, but he knew enough to keep things short. Einstein once told a commencement audience, "I do not have any particular thoughts to express today, so I wish you all success in your future years." He then sat down.

Maybe there's a lesson in that.

Dedications: Buildings, Monuments, Parks

Groundbreaking; Cornerstone Laying; Opening Day

When we build, let us think that we build forever
John Ruskin

The township builds a new senior center. The university dedicates a new monument. The state opens a new park.

If you're the person who's responsible for saying a few words at the dedication ceremony, ask yourself some basic questions before you prepare your remarks:

Where Will the Dedication Take Place?

In 2004, former First Lady Nancy Reagan unveiled the U.S. stamp honoring former President Ronald Reagan at the Reagan Library in Simi Valley, California—a fitting location to make the tribute.

Who Cooperated on the Project?

Find out the names of key leaders, planners, and supporters, and thank them for their cooperation. For example:

There's a Roman proverb that says, "A strong city can only be built by brother helping brother." And that was certainly the case when we built this new YMCA for our community. Many people helped to turn our dream into reality, and I'd like to thank them now.

Notify those people in advance, so they're ready to raise their hands or stand up when their names are mentioned.

Would Major News Events Require Mention?

The opening of the New Hope-Solebury Upper Elementary School in Pennsylvania took place when media coverage of the tsunami disaster riveted public attention. The school superintendent raised the American flag so students could offer their pledge of allegiance—and then lowered the flag to half-mast in honor of tsunami victims.

Who Will Attend the Event?

Publicists like to joke, "Give me a couple of weeks, a couple of spotlights, and a couple of celebrities, and I can make a grand opening for just about anything."

The mere presence of some "big names" will create special interest for your ceremony. Know who will attend, what they're famous for, how they contributed to the effort. Think about why they're important to the community, and how they can serve as role models for the audience. Mention a few of these details in your speech.

Will Anyone Else Speak?

I once attended the dedication of a civic center where one of the officials seemed to forget the presence of other speakers. While he rambled on for 25 boring minutes, the audience became increasingly restless—and the other speakers became increasingly worried.

Thou shalt not steal another speaker's time.

Would Music or Art Enhance the Event?

When the new Holocaust Museum opened in Israel in 2005, leaders from around the world gathered to honor the museum with their good words. Perhaps the most moving tribute? Photographs of Holocaust victims, shown in the background while a chorus sang.

Is There a Suggested Theme for the Event?

Will the ceremony revolve around a central theme? Will it be tailored to a specific public relations objective? If so, you'll want to know about that.

Try to be more profound than Calvin Coolidge was on one occasion. When the president was asked to break ground for a public building, he merely pointed to the broken earth, said "That's a mighty fine fishworm," and left.

Chances are, your audience will expect something more substantial.

Will the Event Be Outdoors?

In 2005, New York City opened the Gates, which consisted of 7,500 orange fabric "gates" that brought Central Park to life for 16 days in the middle of winter. How to launch a major outdoor art event in such cold weather? Like a "happening." In the festive spirit of a Woodstock-type event, Mayor Michael Bloomberg took a sixties approach: "Welcome to New York, and let your mind expand."

Also in the winter of 2005, San Francisco heralded the art opening of the season: the Solid Waste Transfer and Recycling Center—44 acres of artistic inspiration, better known as "the dump." Approximately 500 gallery goers attended—along with an uncounted number of seagulls.

What Does the Building Signify?

When the Hubert H. Humphrey Building was dedicated, Senator Humphrey himself set the tone with these remarks:

> It was once said that the moral test of government is how that government treats those who are in the dawn of life, the children; those who are in the twilight of life, the elderly; and those who are in the shadows of life—the sick, the needy, and the handicapped.

Will a Plaque or Other Memento Mark the Dedication?

Two years after the *Challenger* disaster, the space shuttle *Discovery* was moved to Cape Canaveral's launch pad in an upbeat ceremony designed to boost confidence and pride in America's space program.

Lt. Col. David Hilmers of the Marine Corps told the cheering July Fourth crowd, "It is a mark of a great nation, of its greatness, that it can rise again from adversity. And with *Discovery*, rise again we shall."

Then Lt. Col. Hilmers was presented with an autograph book that was to accompany the *Discovery* crew on its voyage. The book contained the signatures of 15,000 space agency employees who worked to support *Discovery* "from lift-off to landing."

What Does the Building Represent to Your Community?

Buildings are more than bricks and mortar. They're a reflection of the community they serve. When Dr. William Vincent, president of Bucks County Community College in Pennsylvania, spoke at the dedication of that county's new library, he stated:

The facility we are dedicating today is a monument to what Bucks County stands for. . . . It is a monument of good bipartisan leadership over the years. It is a monument to our fellow citizens who support the life of the mind through their participation, as well as their tax dollars. It is a monument to the human spirit that prevails today among us all and is forever recorded in this repository.

How Will the People in Your Community Be Helped?

Will your new library boost literacy? Will your new retirement center give seniors more dignity? Will your new community swimming pool teach kids to become safer swimmers?

Always point out the *human* benefits of any construction efforts. As Winston Churchill once said, "We shape our buildings; thereafter, they shape us."

What Difference Will It Make in Everyday Life?

At the launching of the *Joshua Appleby* (at the Marinette Marine Corporation in Wisconsin), Adm. James M. Loy spoke of the public service this ship would provide.

Joshua Appleby is well on the way to becoming a beautiful ship, but we're not buying it to look at: We're going to put it to work. *Joshua Appleby* will be a proud member of the Coast Guard's aids-to-navigation fleet . . . the working cutters . . . the ones we paint black so the dirt doesn't show.

One of my priorities as Commandant is to raise the public's awareness of the extraordinary value of the Coast Guard's work.

It is often difficult for those of us who serve in the Coast Guard to realize that most Americans, even those with a strong respect for the military, are simply not aware of the enormous range of services the Coast Guard provides to the public on a daily basis. . . .

The Coast Guard maintains about 50,000 short-range aids to navigation along our coasts and harbors, our navigable rivers, the

Great Lakes . . . and anywhere else commercial, military, or recreational users may need a visual clue as to their whereabouts on the surface of the earth.

Every one of these aids needs to be taken care of. 50,000 aids that need to be placed on precise stations. 50,000 complex systems of electrical and mechanical precision that must function in all weather conditions. 50,000 structures of wood or metal or stone that need to be cleaned and painted so they stand out clearly against the environmental backgrounds.

Coast Guard men and women do that work on cutters like the *Joshua Appleby*.

What High Purpose Will be Served?

President Warren G. Harding spoke at the laying of the cornerstone of the City Club building in St. Louis, Missouri, back in 1923. (Notice how he foreshadows the most famous lines at President John F. Kennedy's 1961 inauguration: "Ask not what your country can do for you. Ask what you can do for your country.")

I like people in the cities, in the states, and in the nation to ask themselves now and then: "What can I do for my city?" not "How much can I get out of my city?"

Has the New Building Been Well Received?

If the librarians were pleased when 1,000 people checked out books on the first day, say so.

If the swimming coach was pleased when 300 kids signed up for swimming lessons at the new pool, say so.

If the curator was pleased when 500 people attended the museum on opening day, say so.

After all, nothing succeeds like success.

What Are the Historical Connections?

Lady Morgan Sydney said, "Architecture is the printing press of all ages, and gives a history of the state of the society in which it was erected."

With this in mind, connect the building with the history, the culture, and the economy it reflects.

Can You Define the Monument?

In speaking at the lighthouse transfer ceremony in Rockland, Maine, Adm. James M. Loy gave this great example to define a lighthouse:

> A lighthouse is more than a building with a light on top of it. A lighthouse is a building with a light *and* a commitment to keep it burning.
>
> There's a big, new pyramid-shaped hotel in Las Vegas with a huge light on top of it. That light is brighter than any lighthouse we have and can be seen farther away than any lighthouse we've ever built. But it is not a lighthouse. Why not? Because there's no commitment to keep it burning. Without the commitment to serve, it's just an interestingly shaped building with a light on it.

What Are Your Personal Feelings?

At the dedication ceremony for JCPenney's Manhattan headquarters, founder James Cash Penney shared his personal feelings: "I wouldn't be human if I didn't feel pride and something that transcends pride—humility."

Well said.

Could You Offer an Inspirational Quotation?

In dedicating a monument at a VA medical center, Brig. Gen. Greg Power said:

One of the more moving tributes I've read was written by a Marine Chaplain—Father Dennis Edward O'Brien. In response to the question, What is a veteran?, here was part of his answer: "He is a savior and a sword against the darkness, and he is nothing more than the finest, greatest testimony on behalf of the finest, greatest nation ever known. . . ."

Would Humor Be Appropriate?

In 2005, President George W. Bush and First Lady Laura Bush attended the dedication of the Abraham Lincoln Presidential Library and Museum in Springfield, Illinois. A longtime admirer of Lincoln, President Bush clearly appreciated the opportunity to participate in this special day. (Indeed, the library's dedication occurred on the same day as the 10th anniversary of the Oklahoma City bombing. President Bush attended the Lincoln Library dedication—sending Vice President Dick Cheney to speak at the Oklahoma City anniversary ceremony.)

Bush received laughter from the crowd with this comment: "In a small way, I can relate to the rail-splitter from out West because he had a way of speaking that was not always appreciated by the newspapers back East."

What Happens If There's Bad Weather?

Each year on December 25th, historical reenactors gather on the Pennsylvania side of the Delaware River to recreate Christmas Day 1776, when George Washington and his army of patriots crossed the river to surprise the British Army in Trenton, New Jersey. Washington's crossing of the Delaware turned the tide of the Revolutionary War.

These annual reenactments depend on the mercy of the weather. But even if storms or ice prohibit safe crossing of the river, much of the event can still take place on land—with spectators appreciating moments like George Washington inspecting the troops.

Of course, sometimes bad weather derails an entire event. The Centennial Celebration for the Riegelsville (Pennsylvania) Roebling Bridge was initially canceled by flooding from Hurricane Ivan. (For all of you history buffs: It was the Roebling Company that also built the Brooklyn Bridge.) The planning committee wisely rescheduled the 100th anniversary ceremony for a later date—giving participants a drier day to enjoy a caravan of antique cars crossing the charming bridge.

EULOGIES

---

*You know, the greatest epitaph in the country is here in
Arizona. It's in Tombstone, Arizona, and this epitaph says,
"Here lies Jack Williams. He done his damn'dest."*
I think that is the greatest epitaph a man could have.

President Harry S. Truman

THE TOUGHEST ASSIGNMENT

Common situations:

- A senior executive dies, and the company's CEO is asked to say a few words at the memorial service.
- A much-loved citizen dies, and the mayor is expected to give a particularly moving eulogy.
- A high school principal dies, and the president of the PTA wants to pay a fitting tribute.
- A soldier is killed in action, and family members want to find the right words to to honor him.

Can they do what's expected of them? Can they prepare an effective eulogy—one that's consoling, inspirational, memorable? Can they organize their thoughts under the pressure of limited time? And can they deliver their tribute under the emotional stress that accompanies a death?

Too often, the answer is no. Eulogies rank among the toughest assignments for speechwriters, clergy, and lay people alike.

A tough businessman once told me, "I've spent all my life standing up to shareholders and customers . . . and I always held my own. But when I had to give the eulogy for a coworker, I thought I was coming apart."

He's not the only one who feels insecure under these circumstances. Even experienced clergy often feel inadequate to give a fitting eulogy.

A minister confided to me, "I once had an older person in my congregation who was so popular and so successful that I dreaded his demise for years. I just didn't think I could offer a eulogy that would do justice to this man. And you know what? When he *did* die, my worst fears came true. I really didn't do a very good job, and I'm sorry to say my eulogy didn't begin to pay tribute to this magnificent man."

If you ever have to prepare a eulogy, I hope these examples will help you do a good job.

Find Words of Faith

William R. Brody, president of The Johns Hopkins University, offered these remarks at the funeral of student Linda Trinh (held at Our Lady of Vietnam Church in Silver Spring, Maryland):

Linda Trinh was Johns Hopkins University at its finest—determined to use her intelligence and faith and insights to advance knowledge in order that she might help other people.

Linda represented the bright promise of tomorrow. She was joyful laughter. She was our best hope for the future.

With you today, all of Johns Hopkins mourns. We have all lost a golden glimpse of the future. We have all lost a treasured daughter.

But we do not despair of hope, remembering Linda's devout faith, and the comforting words of the prophet Micah: "When I fall, I shall arise; when I sit in darkness, the Lord shall be a light unto me."

Not long ago, a physician from Johns Hopkins who served as an Army doctor in Vietnam had a six-year-old son who developed leukemia. After many months of terrible struggle, the boy died. And his father, reflecting that despite their very best efforts they could not save their son, came to realize the only absolutely sure thing in life is the love we can give to others. And so he wrote about his experiences, and in particular, he wrote these final words I can offer, this brief benediction for all parents who grieve:

"May we all find peace in the shared hope that our children who brought us such joy with their short lives are now a host of angels, loving us still, feeling our love for them, awaiting our coming, and knowing that they are safely locked forever in our hearts."

Stress Positive Attributes

President Jimmy Carter included this thought in his eulogy for former Senator and Vice President Hubert H. Humphrey:

According to Gandhi, the seven sins are wealth without work, pleasure without conscience, knowledge without character, commerce without morality, science without humanity, worship without sacrifice, and politics without principle. Well, Hubert Humphrey may have sinned in the eyes of God, as we all do, but according to those definitions of Gandhi's, it was Hubert Humphrey without sin.

Emphasize the Person's Value to the Organization

Vernon Nunn was a beloved administrator who worked at the College of William and Mary for nearly 40 years. Upon Nunn's death, James Kelly, assistant to the president, offered a eulogy that began:

It would be extremely difficult to speak of Vernon L. Nunn and not think of the College of William and Mary. And it's going to be equally difficult to speak of the college and not think of Vernon Nunn. To generations of students, faculty, and staff, the two are inseparable.

Remember the Early Years

When President Richard M. Nixon died in 1994, Senator Bob Dole gave a moving eulogy. Dole drew on the early years of Nixon's life—recalling him as "the grocer's son who got ahead by working harder and longer than anyone else . . . the student who met expenses by doing research at the law library for 35 cents an hour."

Talk About How Much You Miss the Person

At a memorial mass on the 20th anniversary of the assassination of President Kennedy, brother Ted Kennedy included these thoughts in his tribute:

> Inevitably we cannot forget the pain of his loss. On bright summer afternoons at Cape Cod or in this waning season of the year, how often we still think of him in all his vigor and say to ourselves, "We miss you, Jack, and always will."
>
> But in the darkness, we see the stars, and how clearly we see him now. We have known other great men and women in our time, in other countries and our own. Yet there was a spark in him so special that even his brief years and early passing could not put it out.
>
> He made us proud to be Americans, and the glow of his life will always light the world.

Speak Directly to the Deceased Person

When Iphigene Ochs Sulzberger, successively the daughter, wife, mother-in-law, and the mother of publishers of *The New York*

Times, died at age 97, her granddaughter, Susan Dryfoos Selznick, spoke on behalf of the family. She addressed her grandmother directly, saying:

> You were particularly important to these men, who carried on the tradition of *The New York Times*. It was said you were the "hidden power" behind the paper. I remember asking you if that was true, and you said, "Who am I to deny anything nice that people have to say about me?"
>
> And then you winked.

Share an Anecdote

Choose a story that reveals the person's character.

A host of patrons and friends came to pay their respects to Frances Steloff, the legendary founder of the Gotham Book Mart in New York City, who died at 101.

Roger Straus, president of Farrar, Straus & Giroux, offered this insight into Ms. Steloff's bookselling career: "Frances always had some book or author she wanted to press on you. She was not above saying, 'Buy a copy of this book. The author needs the royalty.'"

After a pause, he added, "It's a practice I approve of."

Quote the Deceased

When famous faces from the world of fashion, art, and publishing gathered at the Metropolitan Museum of Art to pay tribute to the legendary fashion figure Diana Vreeland, photographer Richard Avedon brought the house to laughter with this Vreeland quote:

> She used to say, "I know what they're going to wear before they wear it, what they're going to eat before they eat it, and where they're going to go before it's there."

Share Some Literature That Has Special Meaning for the Family

Senior naval officers, members of Congress, and about 1,000 other people gathered at the National Cathedral in Washington to pay final respects to Adm. Hyman Rickover.

Mrs. Rickover had asked former president Jimmy Carter to read from John Milton's "Sonnet on His Blindness."

At first, Mr. Carter said, he was puzzled by the widow's choice. But then he came to realize that the last line of Milton's poem had special meaning for all the wives of submariners who were away at sea: "They also serve who only stand and wait."

Find "Little Details" That Capture the Essence of the Person

I was asked to give the eulogy for Mildred Hess Norton, who had lived her long and spirited life to the hilt. I wanted to capture the essence of her life-loving personality, and I opened this way:

> What can you say about a 98-year-old lady who keeps 20 or 30 bottles of nail polish in her refrigerator at all times, so she can always have the perfect color manicure for any occasion?
>
> What can you say about someone like this?
>
> Mildred Norton was a remarkable woman.

Give the Audience a Chance to Smile

Mourners often welcome the opportunity to enjoy some gentle laughter, to recall a funny incident, to remember the good times. By using a light touch of humor, you can ease their grief and unite the mourners in a shared memory.

When Barry Ashbee, assistant coach of the Philadelphia Flyers, died of leukemia at age thirty-seven, the Reverend John

Casey, chaplain of the team, said, "The Lord has taken him to his place of rest. Let us hope it is a place where he will see nothing but great defensemen and that the ice will always be smooth."

ECUMENICAL SERVICES

Funerals should aim to unite all of the families, friends, and admirers in a shared spirituality that fosters a common bond.

A memorial service for Admiral Rickover, who was born to a Jewish family in Russia-controlled Poland, was decidedly ecumenical. It was held in an Anglican cathedral, with a Roman Catholic priest giving the eulogy, and a Baptist reading an inspirational sonnet. A Jewish, a Protestant, and a Catholic Navy chaplain each lead prayers.

MEMORIAL SERVICES FOR MASS DEATHS

What words of comfort could you offer if several high school students were killed in a car crash on their way to a big football game? If an entire family was killed in a hotel fire while taking a vacation? If a group of senior citizens was killed while making a bus trip?

Mass deaths bring mass grieving, and speakers must take extra care to meet the mourners' emotional needs, to offer a sense of comfort, to provide a sense of community.

Thirty-five students from Syracuse University were killed when Pan Am flight 103 crashed over Lockerbie, Scotland. At a news conference, the chancellor of the university, Dr. Melvin Eggers, said, "We have lost some of our best and brightest. They were talented and beautiful people. It will be hard to express our sorrow."

The university then organized a campus memorial service where more than 10,000 people gathered to share their tragic loss. As speaker Mario Cuomo, then governor of New York, explained it, "We gather here because so great a grief cannot be borne without being shared."

In his address, Governor Cuomo shared an inspirational story from the Talmud about a rabbi and his wife:

> When the wife told the rabbi that a man who gave her two diamonds had come to take them back, the rabbi agreed that she had to return the diamonds to the man. After all, they weren't really hers to keep. Then the rabbi's wife explained: "Rabbi, the Lord gave us two precious diamonds—two wonderful sons. And now he has taken them back to him." Hearing this news, the rabbi paused as tears came to his eyes, and he said, "The Lord gave and the Lord has taken away."

Throughout his speech, Governor Cuomo kept his eyes on the families who had sustained this grievous blow.

As a final farewell, English professor Douglas Unger slowly called the name of each student, ending with this parting: "To all of you, good-bye. Good-bye to our friends and our darlings."

INFORMALITIES

Sometimes, words alone can't express your emotions. Consider:

Bells

How best to pay tribute to Elizabeth the Queen Mother, who died at age 101? By tolling Westminster Abbey's tenor bell once a minute for 101 times—in ringing tribute for each year of the Queen Mother's remarkable life.

Special Flowers

For the Queen Mum's funeral services, florists created displays using blooms specifically chosen from her favorite English flowers.

Music

Music speaks a universal language. Congressman Mickey Leland, who was killed in a plane crash in Ethiopia while aiding the cause of world hunger, was eulogized in a Roman Catholic mass, enlivened by the jubilant sounds of gospel singing and the jazzy strains of a saxophone.

A tribute for Irving Berlin included songs and reminiscences interspersed with film and television clips.

A service for jazz saxophonist Dexter Gordon featured musical tributes instead of the customary eulogies.

Art

At a memorial service for painter Elaine de Kooning, people saw photographs of Mrs. de Kooning taken over a period spanning a quarter century.

Personal Possessions

When 5,000 students and friends attended a memorial mass for Hank Gathers, star forward of the Loyola Marymount basketball team, his teammates paraded through the gymnasium displaying the dead player's jersey.

Candles

At a memorial service for the victims of violent crime, candles were lit in memory of victims, and pictures of victims were taped on posterboards near the altar.

Whimsical Touches

At a celebration of the life of Jim Henson, beloved creator of the Muppets, congregants waved colorful foam butterflies on wands. The wands were distributed with the programs, which included a quote by Mr. Henson: "Please watch out for each other and love and forgive everybody. It's a good life, enjoy it."

A Standing Ovation

When actor Tony Randall died in 2004, the theater community gathered at the Majestic Theater on Broadway to pay tribute. The last speaker of the afternoon was none other than Jack Klugman, who played with Tony Randall in their 1970s television comedy series *The Odd Couple.* Klugman concluded by inviting the crowd: "Let's stand for our friend one more time."

A FINAL THOUGHT

Yes, eulogies say a great deal about the person who died, but they also say a great deal about the person who gives the eulogy.

In the words of William E. Gladstone: "Show me the manner in which a nation or a community cares for its dead. I will measure exactly the sympathies of its people . . . and their loyalty to high ideals."

Speak in a manner that reflects the sympathies . . . and the highest ideals . . . of your entire community.

You only have one chance to eulogize someone. Make it good.

FAREWELLS

Farewell: "A sound which makes us linger."
Lord Byron

Maybe you're moving to a distant state, or transferring to a different division, or accepting a job with another company. Maybe your branch manager is relocating, or changing careers, or leaving to raise a family.

You'll want to say a few words of farewell. How can you capture the right tone, and avoid the emotional pitfalls that often accompany such partings?

IF YOU ARE THE PERSON LEAVING

When William Faulkner quit an early job as postmaster, he wrote this less-than-sentimental farewell:

> As long as I live under the capitalistic system, I expect to have my life influenced by the demands of moneyed people. But I will be damned if I propose to be at the beck and call of every itinerant scoundrel who has two cents to invest in a postage stamp. This, sir, is my resignation.

Well, Faulkner's farewell certainly does have a ring to it, but most of us would probably prefer to make our exits in a less caustic way. Here are some ideas to help you craft a farewell speech that leaves *everyone* feeling good.

Allow Your Supporters to Share the Moment

President Ronald Reagan ended his farewell address to the American people with this emotional tribute to his supporters:

> We've done our part. And as I "walk off into the city streets," a final word to the men and women of the Reagan Revolution, the men and women across America who for eight years did the work that brought America back:
>
> My friends, we did it. We weren't just marking time, we made a difference. We made the [country] stronger, we made the [country] freer, and we left her in good hands.
>
> All in all, not bad, Not bad at all.
>
> And so, good-bye. God bless you. And God bless the United States of America.

Express Your Ties to the Area

Consider the honesty of Abraham Lincoln's farewell to the citizens of Springfield, Illinois, as he departed for Washington:

> No one not in my position can appreciate the sadness I feel at this parting. To this people I owe all that I am. Here I have lived more than a quarter of a century; here my children were born, and here one of them lies buried. I know not how soon I shall see you again.

Thank Your Associates

Mr. Arturo Niimi, as president and CEO of Toyota Motor Manufacturing North America, included this thought in his farewell remarks at the Metropolitan Club in Cincinnati, Ohio:

> I have mixed feelings tonight. On the one hand, it's wonderful to see so many of the people I've gotten to know since moving here

three years ago. On the other hand, it makes me sad to be leaving this community. . . .

I want to take this opportunity to thank all of you for the tremendous support you have given Toyota during my time here. In particular, I want to thank the companies that have become Toyota's business partners.

You deserve a lot of the credit for Toyota's fast growth and amazing success in North America. You are part of our strong supplier base. You are members of Toyota's manufacturing family.

Try Some Gentle Humor

Humor can help diffuse the emotional tension. When Harry Truman left the White House, he quipped, "If I'd known how much packing I'd have to do, I'd have run again."

IF OTHERS ARE LEAVING

Thank Them and Praise Them

Be generous, be specific, be sincere. If someone's work wasn't very successful, try to praise the person's enthusiasm, dedication, or integrity. The point is: when people are leaving, they deserve a good send-off. Find *something* to praise.

As Xenophon said, "Praise is the sweetest of all sounds."

Turn Back the Clock

Are you saying good-bye to an accountant who has served your company since 1990? Recall the highlights of that year: when the word "recession" got a record workout (appearing over 1,500 times in *The Wall Street Journal*) . . . and bumper stickers reflected America's growing frustration with the economy: I GET PAID WEEKLY—VERY WEAKLY.

Try to get old photographs showing the person's early days on staff; back issues of company publications are good sources. Put together a scrapbook or CD. Include shots of colleagues through the years—the more candid, the better.

Offer Personal Remembrances

Ask the person's coworkers and colleagues for some anecdotes. Include a few of these affectionate recollections in your farewell speech.

Cite Professional Accomplishments

If someone boosted sales, or improved morale, or created new programs, say so. Offer details. For example, if someone instituted a drug-treatment program that reduced absenteeism by 25 percent, cite that as a major accomplishment. A few well-chosen details will make a big impression—and create a lasting memory.

Try to Create a Family Feeling

When *A Chorus Line* closed as the longest-running show in Broadway history, Joseph Papp, head of the New York Shakespeare Festival, which produced the musical, walked onstage after the final number and introduced all of the members of the current cast.

Then, one by one, he introduced members of the original cast as they came onstage. He also named the show's creators.

Finally, he said, "This show is dedicated to anyone who has ever danced in a chorus or marched in step anywhere." And, with that, he turned to the casts and asked them to take their final bows.

After a record 6,137 shows, the curtain finally came down on *A Chorus Line*. With Papp's fond farewell, it's hard to imagine a dry eye in the house.

Fund-Raising

Charity begins at home, but should not end there.
Thomas Fuller, MD

Hospitals, colleges, museums, politicians, churches; they all want to improve their fund-raising efforts.

Perhaps your company is supporting a drive for the United Way, or your college is raising money for a special lecture series, or your daughter's softball team is seeking donations to buy new equipment. How can you persuade people to give to your cause?

Emphasize People, Not Materials

Raising money to build a new athletic center? Don't sell the bricks and mortar. Sell the great activities that will take place in the new building.

What will people gain if they contribute to that athletic center? Stress the benefits. Appeal to their own interests.

Put Giving in Perspective

Most people could give a lot more than they do. Some people could give a *whole* lot more than they do. Your job is to motivate them.

An old saying goes, Give till it hurts. But think about it: No one wants to hurt. You'll get better results if you encourage people with a different tack: Give till it feels good.

A German proverb says it best: Stinginess does not enrich; charity does not impoverish.

Engage the Audience with a Rhetorical Question

President John F. Kennedy presented this thought-provoking question when he addressed the Protestant Council of the City of New York (just a few weeks before he was assassinated in 1963):

> Is this nation stating it cannot afford to spend an additional $600 million to help the developing nations of the world become strong and free and independent—an amount less than this country's annual outlay for lipstick, face cream, and chewing gum?

Try a Touch of Humor

When the College of William and Mary held a fund-raising auction in New York, the auctioneer began by teasing the audience "to spend more than you ever intended"—which they did, raising more than $41,000 in just one evening to benefit the college.

Cite Your Own Contributions

Have you given generously to local historic efforts? The audience might appreciate hearing about your contributions. (For example, why do you care so much about restoration projects? How did you first get involved? What makes you keep giving?)

If you're shy about "tooting your own horn," admit your feelings to the audience.

A church member who had contributed generously on many occasions was asked to spearhead an important new fund-raising drive. She felt embarrassed to talk about all the money she had given to the church, and she candidly admitted her discomfort to the congregation: "I'm uncomfortable speaking about my financial gifts to this church, but I hope you take my personal comments in the spirit they're intended." She then spoke about the joy she received from contributing to a church that had brought her so much solace over the years. The congregation sensed her sincerity and responded warmly to her personal message.

Give a Demonstration

Want to involve the audience in your cause? Don't just *tell* them about the benefits of your organization; *show* them. Use props. Let people handle samples, try products or look at photos.

SOME CAUTIONS

Have a Backup Plan

When Anthony Luna, director of development for Pearl S. Buck International, tried to give a PowerPoint presentation at a board of supervisors meeting, his laptop computer did not function. But, he had a wise backup plan: old-fashioned, hard copy of his 12-slide presentation. Luna read through his text with the supervisors—making all of his points, page by page. The upshot? He got the local government grant he requested, plus additional funds.

Avoid Technical Language

I once heard a doctor solicit funds for a new emergency service. He had a terrific cause, but he lost much of the audience by using highly complex medical terminology.

You'll be better off if you put everything in ordinary, everyday language, so ordinary people can understand what you're saying.

Define Unfamiliar Terms

I once heard an activist solicit funds for AIDS research. Unfortunately, she used acronyms throughout the speech—GMHC, DIFFA—and some listeners didn't understand what she was saying. Define each acronym the first time you use it, and don't use so many acronyms that they become confusing.

Avoid Long Sentences and Complex Grammatical Structures

One teacher wrote an elaborate proposal for a new program. Unfortunately, when she gave speeches to drum up interest in her cause, she simply read from that tedious document, turning off audiences with her stuffy, bureaucratic language.

Remember, a speech is designed for the ear to listen to, it's not designed for the eye to read. You've got to keep everything simple, so your listeners can grasp your message.

Taking an elaborate document and reading it out loud does *not* make it a speech. It only makes your audience fall asleep.

Avoid Handing Out Materials While You're Speaking

A priest made the mistake of handing out brochures while he solicited funds for an elder-care center. He then watched in dismay as the audience started reading—and stopped listening.

Distribute supporting materials *after* your speech.

A WORD ABOUT FUND-RAISING GIFTS

Perhaps you'd like to offer gifts to your contributors. Fine—just make sure your gifts are appropriate to your cause. Gifts should enhance your fund-raising message.

Some examples:

- If you're soliciting funds to expand your community library, offer contributors a pair of bookends made from bricks.

- If you're soliciting funds to enlarge your hospital, offer a health-related gift that contributors can use to improve their own well-being. Perhaps you could present donors with a calorie counter, or a poster with first-aid suggestions.

- If you're seeking donations to provide housing for the homeless, offer contributors a personal letter of thanks from one of the homeless people who've benefited. Let contributors feel they've really made a difference.

HONORARY DEGREES

---

*I had not the advantage of a classical education, and no man
should, in my judgment, accept a degree he cannot read.*
Millard Fillmore, declining a degree from
Oxford University in 1855

President Fillmore may have turned down an honorary degree, but most people are thrilled to accept the honor. After all, it sure beats dragging yourself out of bed for eight o'clock classes and burning the midnight oil for exams.

Once honorees find out they'll have to give an address, however, a few doubts start creeping in. Nagging thoughts, such as, Is it really worth all the bother? Maybe I should just decline and say I have another engagement that day.

Yes, it really *is* worth all the bother. And, no, you shouldn't try to wiggle out of it.

If you're fortunate enough to be offered an honorary degree, snap it up—even if you *do* have to give a speech before you can claim the academic title!

Maybe these suggestions will help:

Flatter the Institution

When John F. Kennedy received an honorary degree from Yale University, he praised the institution with these words: "Now I have the best of both worlds: a degree from Harvard *and* a degree from Yale."

Express Deep Appreciation

You're receiving a fine and rare honor, an honor that places you in a very select group. Acknowledge the richness of the moment, and express your deep appreciation.

Express Pride in Your Achievements

You're being honored because the university thinks you've achieved a great deal. Share some of the highlights of your career. What's given you the greatest satisfaction? What stumbling blocks have you encountered and overcome? What tips can you share with that eager audience?

A commencement audience will be looking up to you. Give them something significant to focus on.

When Helen Thomas, chief White House correspondent for United Press International, received an honorary degree from Elizabethtown College in Pennsylvania, she spoke fondly of her job: "I have been very privileged to cover the White House with my ringside seat to instant history. No democracy is possible without a free press and a free flow of information."

Try Some Humor

Remember, there's no law that says you have to be pompous. Surely comedian Chevy Chase should get an A + for the way he accepted his honorary degree at Bard College in New York:

It's customary for a commencement speaker to dole out advice to the graduates as they enter public life. Well, here I go.

Avoid fatty foods.

Avoid smoking and drugs, Bensonhurst, the Gaza Strip, Bungee jumping, humorless people, bad music, fashion, weight training, and hair care products.

Oh, and one more thing.

Never, ever tell the truth. Embellish, patronize, pander; use hyperbole, braggadocio; mollify. But never actually tell the truth. In time, those who know you or who are smart enough will *discern* the truth about you. Your job is to act. Keep the dream alive.

Also, never call me. Thank you very much and congratulations.

IMPROMPTU SPEECHES

It takes three weeks to prepare a good ad-lib speech.
Mark Twain

You know that old saying, The only sure things in life are death and taxes? Well, I'd like to amend it: The only sure things are death, taxes, and being asked to give an impromptu speech.

You see, it isn't a question of "if" you'll be asked to speak; it's only a question of "when."

A staff meeting, a PTA meeting, a professional workshop, a town forum, a school board showdown; you show up thinking you'll just listen, and then someone points a finger at you and says, "Susan, could you stand up and tell us how this program worked for you?"

Well, *could* you stand up and give a good impromptu speech? You'd better, because all eyes will be on you, expecting you to say something that's both coherent and interesting.

Of course, if you're smart, you'll think about your impromptu speech *before* you're called upon. Any time you go to a meeting where there's even the slightest chance that someone might ask you to say a few words, you should gather your thoughts in advance.

Ask yourself some basic questions:

- Who will be in the room?
- What's on the agenda?
- Do I have expertise in any of these areas?
- Are there any controversial topics?

- Who are the scheduled speakers?
- What do I know that might interest them?
- What do I know that nobody else in the room knows?

Make some notes about subjects that may come up. (You should be able to anticipate at least 75 percent of these issues.) Jot down two or three points about important topics.

See if you can find a startling statistic or a compelling example or a catchy quotation, something you can memorize now, then "pull out of the air" when you're asked to speak.

If you practice your responses in advance, they'll be firmly in your mind, ready to use whenever you need them.

WHEN YOU'RE ASKED TO
SAY A FEW WORDS

These seven guidelines should help:

1. *Feel free to pause for a few seconds to collect your thoughts.* Believe me, your silence won't cause the audience to think you're stupid. They'll think you want to give a good answer.

2. *Be decisive.* Once you pick your topic, stick with it. Don't change subjects in midstream.

3. *Open with a general statement.* This will give you some extra time to organize your thoughts, allow you to get used to being on your feet, and allow the audience to get used to your speaking style. If you open with something general—"Alcohol treatment programs do a terrific job helping industry control absenteeism," for example—you'll gain five valuable seconds to compose your response.

4. *Offer just two or three points of evidence.* Don't get bogged down with chronological details. "In May of 2002, or maybe it was June, I'm not sure, it could even have been July, anyhow it

was somewhere around then" is hardly a way to inspire confidence in an audience.

5. *Look at the whole room*, not just at the person who asked you to speak.

6. *Wrap up your remarks with a firm conclusion*, such as a memorable, quotable line that people can focus on. Deliver it with an air of confidence and finality.

7. *Once you've offered your conclusion, don't amend it.* Don't be tempted to add on. Just stop.

HOW TO AVOID OFF-THE-CUFF DISASTER

Suppose, God forbid, someone asks you for an opinion, some advice, a critique, whatever, and you've never given the subject any thought. You're caught totally off guard. Now what?

If you maintain a sense of poise, your audience will accept almost anything that comes out of your mouth. So, keep your chin up, your back straight, your eyes alert, your voice steady, and give a short, simple answer.

Don't embellish. Don't stammer. Above all, don't apologize. If you start saying things like, "Gee, I feel terrible. I didn't know I'd have to say anything. I really don't know much about this topic. I'm so embarrassed . . . ," well, if you say things like that, you'll just make the audience uncomfortable, too.

Maybe you can take some comfort from Abraham Lincoln. After General Lee's surrender was announced, people called for Lincoln to make a speech. The president simply said that he had no speech ready and instead called for a stirring rendition of "Dixie."

Look at it this way: Whenever you're speaking off-the-cuff, no one expects you to sound like you're giving the keynote address at a national convention. Just make a short comment—and quit while you're ahead.

Introducing Speakers

Your audience won't know if you're a bad speller, but they will know if you use or pronounce a word improperly. In my first remarks on the dais, I used to thank people for their "fulsome introduction," until I discovered, to my dismay, that "fulsome" means offensive and insincere.

George Plimpton

Suppose you've been asked to introduce a speaker, and you don't know what to say.

A tough spot? Not really. Just call the speaker and ask for a written introduction—not a basic biography (too general) or a formal résumé (too detailed) or an academic *vita* (too scholarly), but a completely written introduction that's *specifically tailored for that speech.*

Most speakers will be glad to oblige. After all, if they write it themselves, at least they'll get an intro they like!

THE INS AND OUTS OF INTRODUCTIONS

What Should a Good Introduction Include?

A good introduction should include:

- several mentions of the speaker's name
- the speaker's credentials
- the title of the speech.

And it should do this in a friendly, personal way that catches the audience's interest and commands the audience's respect.

And an introduction should *not*—repeat, *not*—sound like a résumé. For example, "In 2001, her responsibilities included————. In 2002 her responsibilities included————. In 2003 . . ."

An introduction should *not* sound like a rehash of the biographical data that's printed on the program. It *should* give some fresh insight into the speaker's interest and expertise in the field.

What If the Speaker Provides You with an Introduction That's Too Boring, Stuffy, or Technical?

Rewrite it to sound more natural. For example, don't recite a long list of professional memberships. Laundry lists put audiences to sleep. Instead, use a lively anecdote that shows the speaker's professional standing.

Don't confuse your audience by using technical language. Why say "The speaker has been employed in the development, design, and effective utilization of methane recovery plants" when you can say, "The speaker has saved our community *x* dollars by turning garbage into gas."

What If the Speaker Gives You an Introduction That's Too Modest?

Add some material that shows the speaker's unique qualifications. What prestigious groups has she spoken to? What recognition has he received? What articles has she published? How much money has he saved the company? Why is she the best person to address the topic?

The more you can establish the speaker as an expert, the better. Audiences like to think they're listening to a real winner.

Some Do's

- Use vivid details that capture the speaker's personality. At the 2005 dedication of a law enforcement training center in Harpers Ferry, West Virginia, Robert C. Bonner (Commissioner, U.S. Customs and Border Protection) introduced Senator Robert Byrd this way:

  The Senator never forgot his roots. He has served the good people of West Virginia for half a century—and has served them exceedingly well. . . .

  In his early campaigns, the Senator himself told voters that West Virginia's best friends were God, Carter's Little Liver Pills, and Robert C. Byrd.

  He has been called West Virginia's "greatest economic-development officer."

  Some have even said that, if he could, he would move the U.S. Capitol to the Mountain State.

- Try to create an emotional bond between the speaker and the audience. Do the speaker and the audience support the same charitable causes or care about the same community concerns? Did the speaker and the audience come from similar backgrounds? Did they have to struggle against the same difficulties? Do they share common values? Now's the time to point out these similarities.

- At the end of the introduction, face the audience—not the speaker—and offer the speaker's name with a sense of finality: "We couldn't have found a more qualified landscape architect than Paul Robertson." Then turn directly to the speaker and smile. If you look pleased and confident, some of your pleasure and confidence will rub off, making the speaker's early moments at the lectern less stressful and more successful.

- In formal situations, applaud until the speaker reaches your side, shake hands, and return to your seat.

- In informal situations, sit down as soon as the speaker rises to speak.

- Pay attention to the speaker's opening. It may contain a reference to you, and you'll want to smile or nod in response.

Some Don'ts

- Above all else: Don't mispronounce the speaker's name! Verify pronunciation in advance. Write the name phonetically, so there's no chance of error.

- Don't try to outshine the speaker. Let the speaker be the star.

- Don't try to cue the speaker. If you say, "I don't know what Marie will talk about, but I certainly hope she gives us the latest results of her new referral program," and if Marie *hadn't* planned to mention that subject, well, then you've created an awkward situation.

- Don't steal the speaker's material. If the speaker told you some startling statistics last week, don't steal the speaker's thunder by citing that data in your introduction. He might have planned to use it in his speech.

- Don't rely on memory. Even if you've known the speaker for twenty years, nervousness might cause you to forget some important details. Use notes for your introduction.

- Don't ad-lib. When you're at a lectern, spontaneity can turn into stupidity with amazing speed—especially if you're giving the introduction after dinner and you've had anything alcoholic to drink. Stick to your prepared comments.

- Don't make grandiose promises, e.g., "This is the funniest speaker you'll ever hear in your whole life." Usually, that's just when the speaker bombs—and you're left looking like a jerk.

- Don't put pressure on the speaker by making comparisons. I once heard a president introduce a new manager by saying,

"Susan has replaced Mike Johnson, who we all know was a terrific speaker. So she's got a hard act to follow." As you can imagine, Susan looked somewhat less than comfortable after that introduction.

- Don't speak too long. When a long-winded chairman introduced humorist Artemus Ward, there was nothing left to say on the subject by the time Ward rose to speak. So Ward began, "The chairman has said all that needs to be said on American wit and humor, so instead of speaking on that subject I shall lecture on Indian meal." And, that's exactly what he did.

- Don't make negative comments. Imagine how the British politician Joseph Chamberlain must have felt when the mayor prefaced his introduction of Chamberlain by saying, "Shall we let the people enjoy themselves a little longer, or had we better have our speech now?"

Some Clichés to Avoid

At one time or another; we've all heard:

- "A speaker who needs no introduction . . ."
- "Without further ado . . ."
- "Ladies and gentlemen, heeeeeere's . . ."

Wouldn't it be nice if we never had to hear them again?

MASTER OF CEREMONIES

*When you don't know what you're talking about, it's hard
to know when you're finished.*

Tommy Smothers

A manager was asked to serve as master of ceremonies at a community event, and he wasn't very satisfied with the way he handled his job. He later confided, "Being an MC was sort of like having to stand up and juggle a dozen oranges in front of an audience. I just kept standing there, fumbling everything and waiting for the whole thing to be over with."

Well, that might be an extreme reaction, but it certainly contains an element of truth.

Being a good MC takes a lot of organization, plus a lot of personality. Unless you prepare carefully and rehearse thoroughly, you're going to be in for a hard time.

Here are a few practical tips to make any MC's job easier:

1. *Know your role.* What are you expected to do? What image should you present? Why were you chosen? What did previous MCs do well or poorly? Can you learn anything from their mistakes? Their successes?

2. *Inquire about the speakers and participants.* Will you have to introduce other people? (Be sure you know how to pronounce their names correctly.) Does protocol demand that speakers be introduced in a particular order? Who will provide you with proper introductions for the speakers?

3. *Ask about the schedule of events.* What time frame must you observe? Will participants receive a printed schedule so they'll know the time restrictions they must adhere to?

4. *Learn how to handle mealtime logistics.* Will the event include a luncheon or dinner? Must you speak while people are eating? Who will instruct the waiters on the importance of "silent service"?

5. *Inquire about any prizes or awards.* Who will provide those items? Who will distribute them during the actual event? (Without supervision, prizes might "mysteriously" disappear, leaving you empty-handed at presentation time.)

6. *Plan some informal comments.* Comments that sound spontaneous are often prepared well in advance. Think about your role ahead of time, and have a few good lines up your sleeve. And be prepared for the little glitches that can occur: faulty microphones, nonfunctioning air-conditioning, fumbled notes, the clatter of broken dishes. If you prepare a few clever ad-libs for these inevitable occasions, you'll be less ruffled—and so will the audience.

7. *Prepare a strong ending.* Don't let the program fade away. Wrap it up—firmly, pleasantly, and on time. Thank the appropriate people. Close with a few strong words that will give everyone a positive send-off.

MEETINGS

Meetings . . . are rather like cocktail parties. You don't want to go, but you're cross not to be asked.

Jilly Cooper

Boring, inefficient meetings are a legendary part of American business life.

If you would like to join the legions of people who know how to conduct a lousy meeting—one that ruins morale, wastes time, and accomplishes zip—consider these 19 tips. They're practically guaranteed to run any meeting into the ground.

NINETEEN WAYS TO RUIN YOUR NEXT MEETING

1. Pick a Rotten Date

Don't consult a calendar. Don't think about colleagues' work schedules. Don't try to accommodate travel plans. Just plunge right in and pick a date—*any* date. For a role model, emulate the organization that mindlessly scheduled an important meeting for the start of Rosh Hashanah—and then wondered why several key people didn't attend.

2. Pick a Rotten Place

Don't visit any meeting sites in person. Don't demand a comfortable, quiet environment. Just pick a spot—*any* spot. When the hotel manager tells you over the phone, "Hey, you really don't need to come all the way over here to check it out. It's a great room. You can take my word for it"—go ahead, believe it. So what if you wind up next to a marimba convention?

3. Position the Tables and Chairs So Everyone Feels Crowded

If a knowledgeable meeting planner tells you to allow 15 square feet per person for classroom-style seating, just disregard that suggestion. Throw in as many chairs as possible. Don't worry about allowing enough elbow room, so people can put notepads on the tables. After all, if you make the meeting boring enough, no one will want to take notes anyway.

4. Don't Bother to Test the Mike in Advance

It's much more disruptive to wait until the room is filled—at which point you can tap the mike repeatedly and drive the audience nuts by saying, "Is this mike working? Is this mike working? Is this mike working?" If possible, strive to create at least a few screeching sounds in the process.

5. Don't Bother Adjusting the Thermostat

Hotels are infamous for keeping their meeting rooms hot and stuffy. But who cares if the audience falls asleep in the middle of your presentation? They probably won't miss much anyway.

6. Don't Notify the Switchboard

When people call the hotel to ask about your meeting, God forbid they should get a well-informed receptionist who could actually tell them the correct time and location. And while you're at it, forget to put a sign in the lobby. That way, prospective attendees can have the pleasure of wandering endlessly through the halls, looking for an obscure meeting room. And that way, you can have the pleasure of latecomers straggling into your meeting and disrupting everyone's attention.

7. Start Late

Ah, always guaranteed to put people in the right frame of mind, and to set the tone for an efficient, productive couple of hours— or days!

8. Make Sure No One Knows the Real Purpose of the Meeting

Written agendas? Who needs them? Look at it this way: If you don't have a clear-cut goal, at least no one can accuse you of failing to reach it. You can also prepare your own hidden agenda. Then, you can have the satisfaction of slipping stuff past the other attendees.

9. Don't Even Bother Thinking About Who Will Introduce You

When you're busy preparing a presentation, you just don't have time to worry about something as trivial as a proper introduction, right? Oh, well, someone will probably be able to introduce you. Somehow. Maybe. If you're lucky.

10. Don't Worry About Making Your Speech Interesting

People are used to boring presentations. One more won't kill them.

11. Don't Worry About Organizing Your Material

It's easier to ramble. And who knows? Maybe people will mistake your disorganization for spontaneity.

12. Throw In As Many Statistics As Possible

If three statistics would do the job, give 'em 30, just for good measure. That ought to impress them.

13. Don't Offer Handouts

Helpful handouts take a lot of work to prepare. Why bother?

14. Throw Around Generalizations

No need to back them up with any details. Of course, some people might wonder how you came up with your conclusions, but hey, you can't please all the people all the time.

15. Kill the Audience with PowerPoint

Lots and *lots* of PowerPoint. In small type size. Right after lunch. All in a nice, dark room, so people can drift into unconsciousness more easily.

16. Make Negative Comments About Other People's Ideas

That's a surefire way to stifle dialogue.

17. Ignore Tough Questions

If anyone doubts your facts, just get huffy. People who don't automatically agree with you can't know much.

18. Allow the Bigmouth in the Second Row to Monopolize the Meeting

You know who I mean: the person who asks a million questions and offers a million comments and never lets anyone get a word in edgewise. Allow this person to jump in with a comment or interrupt with a question whenever he feels like it—even as the rest of the audience grows resentful and impatient.

19. Try to Waste As Much Time As Possible

If a five-minute presentation would accomplish your goals, what the heck, stretch it to 15, so you can look more "impressive." If you run into another speaker's time—tough. If you make the meeting run late—too bad. People love to complain about long, boring, useless meetings. Might as well give 'em something to complain about, right?

PANEL PRESENTATIONS

Conversation: "The last flower of civilization . . . our account of ourselves."

Ralph Waldo Emerson

George Bernard Shaw was once invited to speak at a seminar, where he was the last in a long lineup of speakers. After receiving a round of applause from the audience, he put the speech-weary audience out of their misery: "Ladies and gentlemen, the subject is not exhausted, but we are" . . . and sat down.

Here are some tips to keep you from exhausting both the audience and yourself.

IF YOU ARE ASKED TO MODERATE A PANEL

- Seat all the panelists at one time, just a few minutes before the presentation starts. You want to give them enough time to get comfortable and put their papers in order, but *not* enough to become restless or anxious.
- Provide each panelist with a glass of water. (It's better to pour these in advance.) Provide extra pitchers for refills.
- Make sure each panelist can see the clock.
- Make sure the room is comfortable. Find the thermostat and set it back a few degrees, if necessary. The last thing you want is a room that's hot and stuffy.

- Use large name cards to identify the panelists, by their first and last names.

- Start on time. Punctuality has been called the soul of business for a reason.

- Introduce yourself right away. Talk about your interest in the subject. Explain the purpose of the panel presentation. Is it a "first," or an annual event? Are the panelists colleagues or competitors? What makes the subject newsworthy?

- Explain the program's structure: speaking order, number of minutes per panelist, time for rebuttals and questions from the audience, distribution of handouts, sales of books, and so on.

- As you introduce the panelists, use each person's name several times. (See Introducing Speakers, page 82 for helpful tips.)

- Encourage the panelists to take a conversational approach. How would they talk at the office, among colleagues, or at the local coffee shop, among friends? Let the audience feel as if they're eavesdropping on an intelligent conversation.

- Give the panelists a 30-second signal so they can wrap up their presentations on time. One effective technique: Display a 3×5 card that reads 30 SECONDS. A visual reminder is less disruptive than a verbal reminder.

- If panelists ignore your 30-second signal, interrupt them politely, but firmly, and give them 15 seconds to finish.

- *Do not* let any panelist run overtime. It's unfair to the other speakers, and unfair to the audience. What's more, it undercuts your authority as moderator. In a strong, steady voice, say, "Thank you, Mr. Jones, but your time is up." Do not apologize for taking a firm stand. If any apologies are due, it's the long-winded panelist who should apologize—to you, to fellow panelists, and to the audience.

- Close the panel presentation on schedule with a few words of thanks to the speakers and the audience.

IF YOU'RE A PANELIST

- Prepare for the worst. Inexperienced moderators may not know the above guidelines; lazy moderators may not bother to observe them. Just try to make the best of the situation.

- Ask to speak first. Don't be embarrassed to ask for the best spot; moderators will usually honor your request. If the other panelists didn't know enough to select a good spot on the program—well, maybe they should have read this book.

- Make sure the moderator knows how to pronounce your name. (Don't assume—*ask*.)

- If the moderator forgot name cards or only mentioned your name once when introducing you, start by saying "Hello, I'm———."

- If the moderator didn't cite your credentials adequately, offer a *brief* biographical sketch. Emphasize the qualifications that apply to your role on the panel.

- If a long-winded panelist refuses to stop speaking and the moderator seems unable or unwilling to control the situation, assert yourself. Slip a note to the moderator. Slip a note to the speaker. If necessary, interrupt: "Excuse me, but you're going overtime, and we're running very late. Out of fairness to the audience, can we move on schedule?" The audience will be forever grateful. And if inconsiderate speakers feel insulted, well, that's their problem.

- If you're the last speaker and time is running out, give a shortened version of your presentation. It's better to give a shortened version than to stick stubbornly to your original version and lose the audience's attention.

PATRIOTIC CEREMONIES

It is sweet to serve one's country by deeds, and it is not absurd to serve her by words.

Sallust, c. 40 B.C.

Maybe you're a Vietnam War veteran, and you've been asked to say a few words at your town's Memorial Day ceremony. Or you're the president of a local civic organization, and you've been asked to give a short speech on Flag Day. Or you're active in community efforts, and you've been asked to host an Independence Day celebration.

Will you be able to say something patriotic, inspirational, and memorable? Something that will leave your audience feeling positive about their town and country?

You can build a variety of patriotic themes around these ideas:

Explain the Meaning of the Day

In a speech at the Versailles Cemetery in Kentucky, Jack Kain (2005 chairman of the National Automobile Dealers Association) asked the audience:

"What does Memorial Day mean to you?"

A group of schoolchildren was asked this question recently. Their reply: "That's the day the swimming pools open."

Memorial Day is also known for its sales, and because it's a three-day weekend, it's become an ideal time to take the family to the beach.

Not many people stop and think about why Memorial Day was established in the first place. . . .

The White House Commission on Remembrance asked the National Automobile Dealers Association, the organization I chair, to help restore the meaning of "memorial" to Memorial Day. And we enthusiastically said yes. . . .

In this way, in future years, when schoolchildren are asked, "What does Memorial Day mean to you," they will *first* say, "It's to honor those who've fallen in the fight for freedom." And the *second* thing they may say is, "It's also when the swimming pools open."

Define Patriotism

Maybe you'll want to quote someone famous. Calvin Coolidge once said, "Patriotism is easy to understand in America; it means looking out for yourself by looking out for your country."

Or, maybe you'd rather define the concept in your own words. What does patriotism mean to you, in *your* community, today?

Make patriotism *active*. Think "verb," not "noun."

What do patriotic people *do* to make their nation safer and their community better?

Talk About the Flag

Woodrow Wilson once described the American flag as "the emblem of our unity, our power, our thought and purpose as a nation."

What does it symbolize for you?

Maybe you can share some personal recollections. Have you ever fought in battle? When you were a kid, did you help your parents display the flag on holidays? Did you ever march in a patriotic parade? Audiences like it when you share these slice-of-life memories.

Praise Peace

Elie Wiesel once defined peace as "our gift—to each other." If your community faces difficult problems, commit yourself to finding peaceful solutions.

Praise Freedom

When President Ronald Reagan gave an Independence Day speech in Decatur, Alabama, he praised America as a land of the free: "No one immigrates to Cuba or jumps over the wall into East Berlin or seeks refuge in the Soviet Union."

Refer to a Nearby Inscription

Does your library, state capitol, or courthouse have an inscription above its entrance? Many do—and they're good starting points for patriotic sentiments.

For example, these words are carved on a plaque at Union Station in Washington, D.C.: "Let all the ends thou aimest be thy country's, thy God's and truth's. Be noble and the nobleness that lies in other men—sleeping but not dead—will rise in majesty to meet thine own."

The following words appear over the doors to the Brooklyn Public Library at Grand Army Plaza: "The Brooklyn Public Library, through the joining of municipal enterprise and private generosity, offers to all the people perpetual and free access to the knowledge and the thought of all ages."

Local inscriptions such as these can create the basis of an inspirational theme.

Praise the Beauty of Your Land

Proud of the rolling hills, the fertile farmland, the majestic mountains? Say so.

Encourage a Broad Outlook

George Santayana once wrote, "A man's feet must be planted in his country, but his eyes should survey the world."

You can use patriotic ceremonies as a time to express cooperation with other peoples.

Foster Unity

Now is not the time for political one-upmanship. Leave party prejudice at home. Concentrate on shared concerns. As New York City mayor Fiorello La Guardia once put it, "There is no Republican or Democratic way to clean the streets."

State Your Pride in Your Government

Stress the positive. In the words of Winston Churchill, "Democracy is the worst form of government that man has ever devised, except for all those other forms that have been tried from time to time."

Express the Need for Defense

President Gerald R. Ford, addressing a joint session of Congress, talked about the strong need for defense:

> A strong defense is the surest way to peace. Strength makes détente attainable. Weakness invites war, as my generation—my generation—knows from four very bitter experiences. Just as America's will for peace is second to none, so will America's strength be second to none.

3021900024 5738

9/11 TRIBUTES

At a 9/11 remembrance ceremony, Senator Carl Johnson, New Hampshire State Senate, told his Meredith, New Hampshire, audience:

> Since 9/11, much has been said about how easy it is for people to be in the *wrong place at the wrong time*.
>
> But if we were listening carefully, there is another lesson—a lesson just as powerful to come from that fateful day.
>
> It's part of the very fabric of our nation. It can be found in the heart of every one of its citizens.
>
> The lesson is this: As Americans, we are far more likely to be in the right place at the right time.
>
> To do a good deed . . . to help those in need . . . to show compassion . . . to lend a hand to a worthy cause.

Arthur G. Stephenson, director, NASA Marshall Space Flight Center, spoke to both civil servants and contractors on the one-year anniversary of 9/11. His remarks were given at Morris Auditorium in Huntsville, Alabama.

> On September 11, 2001, enemies of freedom sought to dim the light of hope that America has shone for decades. Those who sought to make us afraid . . . have only reminded us what it means to be brave. Those who tried to hurt us . . . only began to heal us by bringing our Nation together in a new way.
>
> It is true that September 11 left its mark on us. But I submit to you, we have left our own mark on September 11. We have become stronger. We came together—united we stood—united we still stand—regardless of race, color, ethnicity, lifestyle, or gender.

When Brig Gen. Timothy D. Livsey spoke to Financial Professionals Incorporated, he shared this insight:

Our military's mission is to protect and defend the United States of America. Since September 11th, there can be no security in our homeland when terrorists are given free reign throughout the world. Franklin Delano Roosevelt warned of this simple strategic reality the day after the attack on Pearl Harbor. He said, "There is no such thing as peace and security in a world ruled by the principles of gangsterism."

VETERAN'S DAY

Connect with the Audience

Notice the effective "you-oriented" approach taken by Lt. Gen. Bruce Carlson when he spoke at the American Legion Lowe-McFarlane Post 14 in Shreveport, Louisiana:

> Some of you in this room today defeated an axis fueled by man's darker angels in World War Two. Some of you served under General MacArthur in Korea. Others answered the president's challenge to "ask not what your country can do for you, but what you can do for your country" and fought in Vietnam. Still others manned freedom's ramparts during the cold war, and others expelled a ruthless dictator from Kuwait during Desert Storm. All of you served a cause that's greater than all of us—the cause of freedom.

Cite Compelling Statistics

Gen. Hal M. Hornburg, Commander of Air Combat Command, honored Veteran's Day 2004 on the steps of the Sandusky County Courthouse in Fremont, Ohio:

> Since World War One, more than one million veterans have been wounded while serving our nation. Many continue to receive

treatment for battlefield injuries and mental trauma they suffered decades ago in battles few of us can remember, but they can never forget.

Our nation rose to greatness on the strength of their service, and their stories are woven into the fabric of our nation's history. Because of their sacrifices, we are free to live, to work, and to raise our families as we please. . . .

We owe them an incredible debt.

Use an Inspirational Quotation

Secretary of the Navy Gordon R. England opened his 2004 Veteran's Day speech by quoting President Reagan:

America is not just a place; rather, it is an ideal, a profound ideal that all people should live in freedom and liberty. These are not innate rights. Freedom and liberty have to be earned, protected, and defended by every generation. As President Reagan said, "Freedom is never more than one generation away from extinction."

For two-hundred and twenty-nine years, American of all races, colors, creeds, and social positions have stepped forward in time of need to protect this idea.

PRAYERS

Work as if you were to live a hundred years. Pray as if you were to die tomorrow.

Benjamin Franklin

Banquets, commencements, award ceremonies, inaugurations, and building dedications often require someone to say a prayer.

If you are asked to give a prayer, can you say something inspirational, gracious, and dignified—something suitable for a public event that recognizes a diversity of religious beliefs?

These eight suggestions should help:

1. Acknowledge the Need for Prayer

When President Abraham Lincoln proclaimed National Fast Day in 1863, he addressed the country's need for prayer this way:

> We have been the recipients of the choicest bounties of Heaven. . . . We have grown in numbers, wealth, and power, as no other nation has ever grown. But we have forgotten God. Intoxicated with unbroken success, we have become too self-sufficient . . . too proud to pray to the God that made us!

2. Thank God for Your Blessings

A wise Yiddish saying goes, *Ven me zol Got danken far guts, volt nit zein kain tseit tsu baklogen zich oif shlechts.*; "If we thanked God for the good things, there wouldn't be time to weep over the bad." A public prayer allows you to bring people together by counting your communal blessings.

3. Ask God to Help You Serve Others

When President George Herbert Walker Bush delivered his inaugural address to the American people, he said, "My first act as president is a prayer—I ask you to bow your heads." Then he offered these gracious words:

Heavenly Father, we bow our heads and thank you for your love. Accept our thanks for the peace that yields this day and the shared faith that makes its continuance likely. Make us strong to do your work, willing to heed and hear your will, and write on our hearts these words: Use power to help people.

For we are given power not to advance our own purpose nor to make a great show in the world, nor a name. There is but one just use of power, and it is to serve people. Help us remember, Lord. Amen.

4. Pray for Strength During Difficult Times

An old saying goes, Pray that you may never have to endure all that you can learn to bear. During difficult times, a prayer for strength is both appropriate and welcome.

5. Use an Inspirational Quotation

When evangelist Billy Graham was asked to give the invocation at the inauguration of President George Herbert Walker Bush he cited this quotation by George Washington: "America stands on two great pillars—faith and morality. Without these, our foundation crumbles."

By quoting the father of our country, Billy Graham tapped into our sense of history and created a shared bond.

Make sure your quotation appeals to a wide cross-section of people. Good choices: bipartisan and interfaith leaders. Their wide appeal will make the entire audience feel included and respected.

6. Commit Yourself to a Noble Cause

Use your prayer to make a commitment, to take responsibility, to move people into action. Heed the advice of Francis Cardinal Spellman: "Pray as if everything depended on God, and work as if everything depended on man."

7. Express a Willingness to Travel in New Directions

A prayer can express your desire to change, to move into new areas, to make a fresh start.

8. Use Candor

Having a rough time? Dealing with some difficult people? Facing a tough situation? Candor may help your prayer cut through the clutter.

After the U.S. Senate finished a marathon session that ran more than 17 hours and exhausted everyone's patience, the Reverend Richard Halverson offered this candid prayer when the Senate returned to work:

Father in heaven, with unbounded gratitude we praise thee for the incredible political system we inherited from our forebears. It is slow, tedious, inefficient; it tries our patience, sets our nerves on edge, frustrates us, rouses our anger and exhausts us; but we would not trade it for any other system.

A FEW CAUTIONS

Don't Be Stuffy

Prayer has been called "a conversation with God." So keep your language conversational, simple, and easy for the audience to understand.

Don't Give a Sectarian Prayer at Public Gatherings

If you give a prayer that's decidedly Christian, for example, you will make other believers feel excluded—and exclusion is certainly *not* the purpose of a public prayer.

When Timothy Healy served as president of Georgetown University, he ordered references to the Trinity eliminated from compulsory university functions. His rationale? "If you're going to say a grace over a mixed dinner, why not say one that everyone can join in."

Indeed.

Don't Pray Too Long

Remember, you're supposed to give a prayer, not a sermon. If you make your prayer too long, the audience may become restless. There's an old German proverb: The fewer the words, the better the prayer.

Don't Use the Same Prayer on Every Occasion

Audiences overlap more often than you might think. If you keep repeating the same prayer at different functions, believe me, people *will* notice. And they will wonder why you don't care enough to prepare something new.

Don't Worry About Giving a "Perfect" Prayer

Perfection isn't your goal; sincerity is. As Gotthold Lessing said, "A single grateful thought toward heaven is the most perfect prayer." Keep that in mind and you'll do just fine.

WHEN WORDS AREN'T ENOUGH

Sometimes the best prayer isn't a prayer. Consider these inspirational options:

Poetry

Perhaps reciting a poem would create the sense of intimacy you're looking for.

Music

When representatives of Jews from around the world gathered at Wannsee Villa in West Berlin, the site where officials of the Third Reich had met decades earlier to plan the Nazi genocide, no prayers were spoken. Instead, participants chanted the Hebrew hymn, "Ma'amin, Ma'amin," declaring faith in the coming of the Messiah.

Silence

Silence is often more eloquent than words. As Bishop Fulton Sheen once said, "Prayer begins by talking to God, but it ends by listening to him. In the face of Absolute Truth, silence is the soul's language."

Amen.

Question-and-Answer Sessions

It is better to ask some of the questions than to know all the answers.

James Thurber

Let's say you've just given a terrific speech. The audience paid attention and gave you a big round of applause. Now that it's over, you can gather your notes, leave the lectern, and relax. Right?

Not so fast. Sometimes, giving a speech is only half the battle; a question-and-answer session might still remain. And if you don't prepare as carefully for your Q&A as you did for your speech, you could be headed for an awkward time.

The fact is, a question-and-answer session can make or break your speech. So plan to make Q&A work for you, not against you.

Here are some general guidelines:

Remind Yourself: There Are No Dumb Questions

Take a good breath and welcome each question. An audience will sense your cooperation and good spirits. Your overall attitude will help you to sell your message—regardless of whatever individual questions might come your way.

Alfred North Whitehead put it in perspective: "The 'silly question' is the first intimation of some totally new development."

Take Questions from All Parts of the Audience

If you overlook the rear of the room, those people will feel left out. Also, if you take too many questions from one person, everyone else will feel excluded—and annoyed.

Be sensitive to issues of gender and age. Don't ignore or patronize.

Listen Carefully to Each Question

Try to remain neutral as you listen. Avoid excessive smiles or frowns. If you react too soon, you'll upstage your own answer. Some speakers get nervous and nod repeatedly, just to show they understand. Don't do this. The audience might mistake your nodding as a sign of agreement.

Pay Attention to Body Language

If you fidget, the audience will sense your discomfort and think you've got something to hide. Don't play with a pen or jingle jewelry. (If you don't trust yourself, remove such items from your person before you speak. After all, you can't click a pen if you don't have one!)

Treat Each Questioner as an Equal

Some speakers automatically respond by saying, "Good question." Don't. After a while, "good question" sounds boring. Even worse, it suggests that other questions *weren't* so good. Also, don't brush off questions from your subordinates and fawn over questions from your superiors. Audiences are quick to spot this attitude—and slow to forgive it.

Repeat All Positive Questions

This way you make sure everyone has heard the question. It also buys you some extra time to compose your answer.

Reword All Negative Questions

This allows you to set the tone and control the emphasis of your answer. *Don't* repeat any hostile language. For example, if you're asked, "Why do you distribute your funds so unfairly?", you could rephrase it: "Is there a better way to distribute our funds? Let's consider that for a moment." Negative questions inflame listeners and make it harder for you to give a balanced answer. And if you repeat a negative accusation, you might be misquoted as having said it yourself.

Begin by Looking at the Person Who Asked the Question

This builds rapport. Then make eye contact with others around the room as you answer so everyone feels involved.

Respond Simply and Directly

If you make your answer too complex, the audience might think you're trying to evade the issue.

Tap the Power of Humor

When reporters asked President John F. Kennedy what he thought about the press, Kennedy disarmed the group with laughter: "Well, I am reading more and enjoying it less."

Don't Extend Your Answers

The more you say, the more likely you are to hang yourself. As Calvin Coolidge said, "I have never been hurt by anything I didn't say."

Of course, at times Coolidge carried brevity to extremes. A dinner party guest once asked Coolidge what he did. "I'm the lieutenant governor," he said. "Oh, how interesting," the guest gushed, "you must tell me all about it." To which Coolidge replied, "I just did."

Don't Limit Yourself by Saying, "This Will Be Our Last Question."

What happens if that question turns out to be hostile—or if you give a poor answer? You'd end your Q&A session on a weak note—unnecessarily. It's better to say something like, "We only have a little time left. Any more questions?" Then, if your next question happens to be an interesting one—and if you're satisfied with your answer—you can end the whole session right there. But, if you get a hostile, rambling, or boring question, or if you give a weak answer, you still have the leeway to take another question and try again.

SPECIAL CIRCUMSTANCES

If You Want to "Jump Into" Someone Else's Answer

In November of 2004, the political buzz centered on President George W. Bush and his closest ally in the Iraq War, British Prime Minister Tony Blair: Was Blair just a rubber stamp for Bush? At a press conference, a reporter asked President Bush if he thought of Blair as his "poodle." Not missing a beat, Blair jumped in and quipped to Bush, "Don't answer yes."

If No One Asks You a Question

Maybe the audience is too shy, too bored, or too unfamiliar with your topic to ask a question. Who knows? But, there's one thing you *do* know: As a speaker, you can't just stand there and let an uncomfortable silence put a damper on your presentation. So ask *yourself* a question. Try, "Earlier today, one of your members asked if I'd address the issue of teacher certification. Let me get to that now." Or, "Last week, when I spoke to the Lion's Club, several people asked me to talk about our funding for the new senior center. That question seems to be on a lot of people's minds, so maybe I should answer it for you, too."

If Someone Asks About Something You Already Addressed in the Speech

Maybe the person was daydreaming; on the other hand, maybe you weren't clear enough. It doesn't matter. Give him or her the benefit of the doubt and answer the question. But approach the topic in a new way so you don't bore the rest of the audience. For example, if you used statistics to illustrate this point in your speech, try using anecdotes or examples to clarify the issue in your Q&A session. If the audience didn't grasp your first approach, maybe they'll understand your second.

If Someone Repeats a Question That's Already Been Asked

Don't answer it. Time is too precious to indulge in this sort of repetition. Say, "I believe we've already taken that question." Then move on.

If Someone Asks a Totally Irrelevant Question

Your marital status, religion, politics, age, finances, your personal life shouldn't concern the audience. If someone hits you with an inappropriate question—"I'm curious. Whom did you vote for in the last election?"—you don't have to answer. In fact, you *shouldn't* answer. Be firm. Say, "That's not what we're here to discuss today." Don't be embarrassed. The person who asks a question like that is the one who should be embarrassed.

When a reporter once asked actress Jaclyn Smith about her financial standing, she dismissed the question quite graciously: "If you're asking me if I'm worth $15 million, I never discuss money. That's my Southern upbringing. We never discuss money, politics, or religion."

If Someone Asks a Truly Inane Question

Give a brief answer—and then go on to another question.

If Someone Asks a Rambling Question

Pick one element and respond to that. (Naturally, pick the element that interests you the most and allows you to give the best answer.)

Remember: When in doubt, don't say any more than you need to. Reporters once asked tenor Enrico Caruso what he thought of Babe Ruth. Caruso said he didn't really know because, unfortunately, he had never heard her sing.

If Someone Tries to Turn a Question Into a Speech

Nip this in the bud. Be polite but firm. Interrupt the person. Ask him or her to come to the point and state the question "in the interest of saving time." When you interrupt the questioner, raise your hand in front of you in a "stop" signal. This gesture will reinforce your words. And believe me, the audience will really appreciate your firmness. Audiences hate it when one person is allowed to monopolize a Q&A session.

It Someone Tries to Squeeze You into a Position

Don't let anyone manipulate you into a certain position, or use innuendo to back you into a corner. Define your own position in clear, direct terms.

A member of the clergy once told Abraham Lincoln that he hoped "the Lord was on our side." President Lincoln stopped this line of questioning with a few blunt words: "I know that the Lord is *always* on the side of the *right*. But it is my constant anxiety and prayer that *I* and this *nation* should be on the Lord's side."

If You Don't Know the Answer

Say so. No one expects you to know everything. Try, "I don't know. But I'll go to the source and find out. If you leave me your name and number, I'll be glad to get back to you with that information by tomorrow."

Note: Don't just say, "I'll get back to you." Questioners take that as a brush-off. Instead, always provide a respectable time frame—and cite any reasons that will clarify your delayed response. For example: Offer to get back to the person "by the close of business today" . . . or "by next Monday morning, when we will have our new manager in place" . . . or "on the 31st of this month, when the complete sales figures will be available."

If You Run Out of Time

Say you're sorry the time is up, and offer to make yourself available to people who want to pursue the subject further, perhaps during a break or after lunch.

HOW TO HANDLE TRICKY QUESTIONS

Never explain—your friends do not need it and your enemies
will not believe you anyway.

Elbert Hubbard

After you've weathered a number of Q&A sessions, you'll be able to spot the tricky questions, and you'll discover they fall into basic patterns. Once you recognize these patterns, you'll handle the questions more easily and effectively.

It took me years of public speaking experience to learn about tricky questions the hard way. In this section, you can learn about them in just a few minutes. Lucky you!

Study the patterns of these tricky questions before you face your next Q&A:

The Hypothetical Question

Avoid being pulled into "what if' situations. For example, "What if you can't meet the deadline?" They're like bottomless pits. Cut off a hypothetical scenario by saying, "We've spent six weeks working on this assignment, and we've met every single deadline along the way. We're confident we'll complete the project on time."

The Off-the-Record Question

"I know it's not public yet, but would you tell us about your expansion plans—off the record, of course."

Sorry, but there's no such thing as an off-the-record question in a Q&A session. You might think you can trust everyone in the room, but . . .

Assume that any answer you give will appear on the front page of tomorrow's paper. It just might!

The Ranking Question

"Would you name the two biggest challenges facing your corporation?"

If you answer with, "Our two biggest concerns are increased productivity and larger facilities," someone will surely counter with, "What's the matter? Don't you consider diversity to be a priority?" And then you're stuck in a hole.

Don't allow a questioner to force you into an arbitrary ranking system. Say, "Well, we're concerned with a number of issues right now. Let me tell you about a few of our priorities."

When Eudora Welty addressed the Poetry Center of the 92nd Street YMCA in New York City, she was asked to name her favorite American authors. Miss Welty cleverly sidestepped the question by saying she'd rather read Chekhov than anyone else. Well put.

The Nonquestion Question

"I don't see any need for a new training program."

How can you respond to a statement like this without appearing argumentative or defensive? Easy. Convert the statement into a question. For example, "I'm hearing you bring up an important question, and that is, 'Why should we spend all this money on a new training program? What's in it for us?'" Then you can answer the question—and cite all the benefits—without having to knock the person's original statement.

The "A or B" Question

"Which will be more important to the company this year: promoting women or promoting minorities?"

Be careful. Don't get tricked into an unnecessary choice. There's no law that says you have to choose between a questioner's options. Say, "They're *both* important. In fact, our personnel department has a few other priorities, as well. Let me take a few moments to tell you about them."

Note how cleverly President Ronald Reagan avoided the pitfalls of this "A or B" question: When Reagan was asked which team he planned to root for in the World Series, he gave everyone a chuckle by saying, "That's an unfair question. I'm supposed to be president of all the people."

The Open Question

"Tell me about your company." This question is deceptively easy—and that's why so many people fail when they attempt to answer it. When given the opportunity to say everything, they can't seem to pick anything. And so they stammer. Or they say something boring. Or they get foot-in-mouth disease.

Open questions are quite common. You get them when you go on job interviews: "Tell me about yourself."

You get them when you go on sales calls: "Tell me about your product line."

You get them when you go to community functions: "Tell us about your company's business philosophy."

Right now, *before* you're put on the firing line, think about some open questions that might apply to *you*—and come up with some good, short, interesting answers. Memorize them. They'll come in handy, I assure you.

The What-Does-the-Other-Person-Think Question

"Why would your competitors be dropping this product line? Do they have something better up their sleeves?"

Unless you are a professional mind reader, you shouldn't speculate about other people's thoughts.

Let other people speak for themselves. Respond by saying, "You'll have to ask them for their reasons." Then bring the subject back into your domain by adding, "But I'd like to tell you why *we're* so committed to this product line."

The Yes-or-No Question

"Will you have to fire any employees this year—yes or no?"

Never allow someone to push you into a one-word answer. It's *your* Q&A session, and you can answer any way you want. Make the statement in your *own* words.

HOW TO HANDLE HOSTILE QUESTIONS

He who opposes me, and does not destroy me, strengthens me.

Edmund Burke

Sometimes, a Q&A session will turn nasty.

Let's suppose you're the principal of a public high school, and you've just finished speaking to a community group about the role of parents in education. Your speech went okay, but now a hand pops up and an angry voice hits you with this zinger:

How can you stand there and tell parents to be more responsible when *you* have failed in your responsibility to us? Ever since you became principal, test scores have gone down, discipline problems have gone up, and salaries have gone *way* up. Where do you get the guts to come here and lecture us about educational responsibility?

Of course, what's really running through your mind at this point is, How can I respond to this question? And the answer is, carefully. *Very* carefully.

Hostile questions aren't impossible to answer. They just take special skills. Why not learn these skills right now—before you find yourself on the firing line?

Start by giving yourself three basic rights:

1. The right to be treated fairly.
2. The right to stay in control—of yourself and the situation.
3. The right to get your message across correctly.

Never forget, *you* are the invited speaker. You are the person who was asked to say a few words to this group. You are the person who spent hours preparing for this Q&A session. And now that you're here, *no one* has the right to take away your role or obscure your message.

Take a deep breath, keep your feet firmly planted, and concentrate on getting your message across. Don't focus on the person's anger. Don't focus on your resentment. *Just concentrate on getting your message across.*

When you prepare for any Q&A, choose two or three important points that you can express in clear, simple, concise language—one-liners that you can use whenever you're in a tight spot. Memorize them. Use them as "focus statements" when the Q&A gets difficult.

A FEW FINAL CAUTIONS

Don't Insult Anyone's Intelligence

Sorry to say, unthinking speakers do this all the time. Consider this exchange:

Q: Why is the school spending so much money for all that lab equipment?

A: Maybe you don't know what our equipment can do. For example—

Q: Are you saying I'm too stupid to know about your lab equipment?

Don't make the questioner feel stupid or inadequate. Listen respectfully to the question, then say something like, "For the benefit of everyone here, let me just take a couple minutes to explain the equipment in our lab. I'd like to tell you what it can do."

Don't Humiliate Questioners

Try to prevent an exchange like this:

Q: Why didn't you examine the facts more carefully before you planned your budget?

A: You're the one who's ignorant of the facts. I guess you must have been daydreaming, because I stated the facts in my speech today. If you'd been listening, you wouldn't have to ask that kind of a question.

Don't browbeat or embarrass questions. They'll never forget the public humiliation, and they'll never forgive you for it. Nor will the rest of the audience.

Don't Make Idle Threats

I once saw a heckler dominate the Q&A session at an important meeting. The speaker grew increasingly frustrated and said, "I'm going to ask you to sit down in a few minutes."

Naturally, the heckler loved all the attention and kept interrupting the session with long-winded questions. The speaker became visibly frustrated, raising his voice and again threatening, "I'm going to ask you to sit down soon."

Alas, "soon" never came. The speaker never acted on his idle threats, the heckler kept disrupting the meeting, and the audience became increasingly annoyed—not just at the heckler, but at the ineffectual speaker, who couldn't control his own meeting.

If you can't carry out a threat, don't make it.

Don't Criticize a Predecessor's Work

Try to prevent an exchange such as:

> *Q:* Why do you think your program is so much better than the one Mary Smith started? We've been using her guidelines for years.
>
> *A:* Oh, the old program had lots of problems, and that's why I had to get rid of it. For example . . .

Don't criticize someone else's work publicly. Even if the person has left the organization, she may have friends who are still around. They will resent you for knocking her work.

The smart response? Explain that you inherited a good program, but that new information, better technology, increased funding, etc., allowed you to build on your predecessor's foundation.

Never give the impression that you've thrown out someone else's work, or the audience will think you are reckless and arrogant.

RETIREMENT TRIBUTES

―――――――――――

Two weeks ago I went into retirement. Am I glad that's over!
It took all the fun out of Saturdays.

President Ronald Reagan

WHEN YOU WANT TO HONOR SOMEONE WHO IS RETIRING

Salute Their Achievements

Don't just praise them. Praise them for doing specific things. Otherwise, it sounds like you're giving a canned speech you happened to find somewhere. They deserve better than that.

Be Generous

You only have one chance to create a final impression. This is no time to be stingy with praise.

Invite a Special Guest Speaker

Ask yourself, Who could offer a unique perspective on this person's retirement? And then include that speaker in the day's ceremonies.

At the retirement ceremony for Capt. Bruce Stubbs, Adm. James M. Loy cited many achievements of Captain Stubbs's 30-year Coast Guard career. And then he offered this surprise:

In a moment, I'm going to ask Captain Stubbs to join me at the lectern for formal recognition of his service to the Coast Guard.

But first, I want to announce a brief departure from the printed program.

When the relationship between an admiral and an aide works well, it is a uniquely symbiotic exchange of goodwill. . . . Bruce, your mentor and former boss has retired to Maine, but he wanted to offer a personal message at today's ceremony . . . and he wanted to deliver that message in person!

Ladies and gentlemen, please join me in welcoming Admiral John B. Hayes, the sixteenth Commandant of the Coast Guard.

Share Some Behind-the-Scenes Stories

People like to reminisce, so take advantage of this opportunity to share a few good stories that will create camaraderie, foster goodwill, and perpetuate fond memories.

One Caution

Do not say that someone will "replace" the retiree.

In 1777, Benjamin Franklin resigned his position as minister to France and returned home to Philadelphia. His successor at the court of Versailles? None other than Thomas Jefferson.

In greeting the new minister from America, French Prime Minister Count Vergennes said, "Mr. Jefferson, have you come to replace Dr. Franklin?"

And Jefferson replied, "No one can ever replace Benjamin Franklin. I am only succeeding him."

WHEN YOU ARE RETIRING

Express Appreciation for the Celebration

Retirement lunches, ceremonies, and tributes require a lot of hard work and planning. Thank the people who cared enough to give you a good send-off.

Be specific. And be generous.

Acknowledge Your Mentors

How did you get started in the field? Who taught you how to do your job? Did a supervisor give you terrific advice, help you through a tough time, or teach you some specialized skills? Now's the time to acknowledge your debt.

Turn Back the Clock

Did you join the organization back in 1987? Describe the department, the company, the industry in those years. Create a sense of shared history.

Recall Your First Day on the Job

David A. Larson Sr. retired from the U.S. Navy in 2001. When he gave his retirement speech at the London Headquarters Building of U.S. Naval Forces/Europe, he recalled his first day of service:

> In October 1969, I stood at the Navy and Marine Corps in-processing center in Albuquerque, New Mexico, as a very scared—yet excited—young man. . . . Four years of my life were about to be given to the Navy and the Nation—this is a lifetime to a twenty-year-old. The most important thing I thought about was, do not make any mistakes. Then someone walked into the room of

pimple-faced kids and yelled, "Attention on deck!" Every set of heels in that place promptly clicked together—*except mine*. In less than a second, the following thoughts went through my mind:

- *Oh no*—my first mistake—don't look around with your eyes— that gives it away immediately you were the person who did not click their heels. Someone must be watching for that.
- Then I thought, How did everyone else know to do that? My recruiter forgot to tell me.
- Should I click them now—even if late—what do I do? I chose not to click them and learned my first military lesson: You can get lost in a crowd.

Be Candid

When Walter Wriston retired as chairman of Citibank Corporation, he offered this observation: "When you retire, you go from who's who to who's what."

Offer Personal Observations

Gen. Douglas MacArthur shared these thoughts upon leaving fifty-two years of military service:

The world has turned over many times since I took the oath on the plains at West Point . . . but I still remember the refrain of one of the most popular barrack ballads of that day, which proclaimed that old soldiers never die, they just fade away. And like the old soldier of that ballad, I now close my military career and just fade away, an old soldier who tried to do his duty as God gave him the light to see that duty. Good-bye.

Use an Inspirational Quotation

Lt. Gen. Philip J. Ford used this quotation at the retirement ceremony for Brig. Gen. Donald Streater at Barksdale AFB:

Robert E. Lee once said that duty is the most sublime word in our language. He said, "Do your duty in all things. You cannot do more. You should never wish to do less."

For Don Streater, devotion to duty included:

- his duty to our Air Force
- his genuine love and caring for our Air Force family
- and, most of all, an unwavering sense of patriotism.

Talk About Your Plans for the Future

Travel? Education? A new sport, hobby, or craft? People will want to hear the details.

Don't just say, "I'll take some college courses." Say, "I've always wanted to visit France, so I'm signing up for French lessons at our community college. Marge and I plan to travel to Paris in April."

Tell a Lighthearted Story

A little bit of humor can help break the tension that often accompanies a retirement ceremony. If you look through the reference materials described in the annotated bibliography, you'll find lots of good anecdotes to use in a retirement speech.

Say You'll Stay in Touch

In an emotional farewell address at the 34th Republican National Convention, President Ronald Reagan said:

> There's still a lot of brush out at the ranch, fences that need repair, and horses to ride. But I want you to know that if the fires ever dim, I'll leave my phone number and address just in case you need a foot soldier. Just let me know, and I'll be there.

Say How You'd Like to Be Remembered

When Beverly Sills retired as chair of the Metropolitan Opera, her 60-year career included many successes: stardom as a diva at the New York City Opera . . . 10 years of managing that opera . . . serving as chairwoman of Lincoln Center.

With all of her triumphs, what made her most proud? "I want to be remembered for what I did on the stage, not behind the stage. If somebody had said to my mother, 'What are you most proud of?' she'd say, 'That voice.'"

Final Thought

Audiences will expect you to look back. But they will not be comfortable if you wallow in the past. In other words: It's okay to look back . . . just don't stare.

SALES/INFORMATION BOOTHS

Beat your gong and sell your candies.
Chinese proverb

Want to hand out literature for your environmental group? Attract customers for your new line of products? Recruit volunteers for your literacy project? If so, you need to know how to run an effective sales and information booth.

A well-run booth is a terrific way to tell people about your organization and gain their support. It's effective, personal, inexpensive, and a great way to keep in touch with the needs of the marketplace, because you receive immediate feedback.

Unfortunately, it can also backfire if you don't prepare carefully. So, use these guidelines as a checklist:

WHAT TO ARRANGE BEFORE THE EVENT

Find an Appropriate Gathering

Some possibilities: community events, professional meetings, college "career days," chamber of commerce exhibitions, trade fairs, conventions, fund-raisers, civic banquets—wherever people gather and have time to linger. Make sure the atmosphere is appropriate for your organization and conducive to conversation. For example, you might be frustrated if you try to run an information booth where alcohol is served or loud music disrupts conversation.

Get an Agreement in Writing

Send the organizers a letter of agreement, and ask them to return a signed copy. Why? Because Tom Smith might say, "Sure, you can set up a table at our civic event," but when you get there, someone else might say, "Sorry, no tables allowed." So write a letter of agreement that states your purpose, when you'll operate the table, and where you'll set it up. Be specific. You don't want to be stuck in an out-of-the-way corner. You need lots of passersby to run a successful booth.

Order Sufficient Supplies

Want to give out brochures that describe your organization? Sell copies of your women's club cookbook? Run a bake sale for the PTA? Distribute consumer checklists? Offer samples of a new product? Make sure you have enough materials. There's no sense in operating a table that's half empty. Preparation is crucial.

Schedule Plenty of People to Work at the Booth

Running a booth is tiring—all that talking and standing around. (That's right; *standing* around. If you're seated, you'll seem less approachable. So the cardinal rule is, no chairs allowed.) Since your staff will need breaks every hour or so, be sure you have enough pinch hitters.

Train Everyone Who Will Work at the Table

A well-informed staff will create a more positive impression, so make sure your people can answer a wide range of questions, not just about your organization, but about the entire event. For example, when the University of Pennsylvania celebrated its 250th anniversary, more than 1,000 volunteers got a wonderful training session—enabling them to answer such practical questions as "Where's the toilet?" and "When does the next jitney leave?"

WHAT TO DO DURING THE EVENT

- Always keep in mind that you have a three-part goal: first, you must get people to stop at your booth or table; second, you must get them to listen to your pitch; and third, you must persuade them to support your cause.

- "Hook" people by having one of your staff stand in front of the table, offering samples or brochures to passersby. Once people stop to accept your items, you can generally engage them in conversation.

- You can also hook people by offering a free beverage or snack. They'll feel obligated to make small talk with you, and then you've got their attention.

- Smile and make everyone feel welcome. (That's one of the reasons why a booth is so tiring. You're constantly "on" as you focus all your attention on other people's needs.)

- Use "ringers." If you hit a slow period, station someone in front of your table to browse through your materials. One customer will attract more customers, but an empty table will turn people off.

- Don't talk with your partners. If people see you talking, they'll feel you're unapproachable. I once approached a table set up by people trying to recruit volunteers to aid the homeless. The two staff members were so busy chatting with each other that they didn't seem to notice me. I felt uncomfortable disturbing their private conversation, so I slipped away and came back ten minutes later. Again, they were having such a grand time talking with each other that they remained oblivious to me and other prospective volunteers. That kind of behavior is foolish and costly. If passersby don't feel welcome at a table, they simply won't linger. And you'll lose a golden opportunity.

- Be sure to get business cards from people. Make comments on the back so you can remember key points about each prospect. For example: "Just joined the firm two months ago," or "Wants to improve her visibility in the community," or "Went to Temple University." Record as many details as possible on each card. These bits of information can serve as conversation openers when you make follow-up calls.

- Never leave a table unattended. You might lose the chance to make a personal connection. And sorry to say, you might also lose your materials. Things such as pens, notepads, and staplers have mysterious ways of walking off. So be visible and alert throughout the event.

WHAT TO DO AFTER THE EVENT

- Follow up.
- Follow up.
- Follow up.

Get the message? Phone people who seemed willing to support your cause. E-mail notices of your next meeting. Give details about a special fund-raising event. Send helpful information to potential customers. Whatever you do, *don't* let your prospects slip away.

SPORTS BANQUETS

If you can react the same way to winning and losing, that's a big accomplishment. That quality is important because it stays with you the rest of your life, and there's going to be a life after tennis that's a lot longer than your tennis life.

Chris Evert Lloyd

Organizing a sports banquet to celebrate a winning season? To honor a terrific coach? To acknowledge the most outstanding player?

Someone will have to say a few words to fit the occasion. If you're the person in charge, maybe you can talk about one of these topics:

Accepting the Responsibility—And Sharing the Glory

Here's Bear Bryant's approach:

I'm just a plowhand from Arkansas, but I have learned how to hold a team together. How to lift some men up, how to calm down others, until finally they've got one heartbeat, together, a team. There's just three things I ever say: If anything goes bad, then I did it. If anything goes semigood, then we did it. If anything goes real good, then you did it. That's all it takes to get people to win football games for you.

The Importance of Teamwork

Red Holzman, the former New York Knicks coach, praised team-work this way:

> On a good team there are no superstars. There are great players, who show they are great players by being able to play with others, as a team. They have the ability to be superstars, but if they fit into a good team, they make sacrifices, they do the things necessary to help the team win.

Share some insights into the special teamwork of your players.

The Value of Building Character

Player's agent Lewis Schaffel once said, "Talent is overrated. You win with character. In a short series, talent might prevail. Over an eighty-two-game [basketball] season, character prevails."

Tell some real-life stories that show the fine character of your players.

A Witty Definition of Your Sport

For example, H. J. Dutiel defined baseball as "a game which consists of tapping a ball with a piece of wood, then running like a lunatic." Oliver Herford called fishing, "The art of taking more fish out of a stream than were ever in it."

You can use irreverent definitions as a springboard to discuss various aspects of your sport.

The Sheer Joy of the Game

Does the smell of a catcher's mitt bring back great memories? Does the sound of a tennis ball hitting the sweet spot seem like music to your ears? Does the sight of a 50-yard pass make you want to stand up and cheer? Share your joy of the game with the audience.

Red Smith expressed his joy of baseball this way: "Ninety feet between bases is perhaps as close as man has ever gotten to perfection."

The Benefits of Sports

Has a strong athletic league been a unifying force in your community? Has victory on the basketball court given your junior high kids something to cheer about? Has a charismatic coach inspired your students to try harder?

If you put athletic victories into *human* terms, your statistics will become even more impressive.

The Wide Appeal of Sports

Almost everybody likes sports. Why? Well, consider this reasoning by Earl Warren, former chief justice of the Supreme Court:

> I always turn to the sports section first. The sports section records people's accomplishments; the front page, nothing but a man's failures.

Previous Winners

Saluting this year's most valuable player? Cite some winners from previous years, and describe how they continue to pursue sports.

The Role of the Coach

What does *your* coach do that makes him special? What contributions has she made? How does he motivate and manage the team?

When Jackie Sherrill was athletic director at Texas A&M, he spoke to alumni groups about his role as head football coach:

> Coaching has changed. Twenty years ago, the coach never left the campus. Now I balance the budget, market the product, do promotions, handle personnel, sell the program, recruit, and coach. Like it or not, it's a different type of business now.

Some Humor

When Green Bay Packer lineman Henry Jordan shared a banquet dais with Vince Lombardi, he joked, "Seriously, Coach Lombardi is very fair. He treats us all like dogs."

The Thrill of Winning

Committed to winning? Then remember Napoleon's advice: "If you start to take Vienna—take Vienna."

Al McGuire, who coached Marquette to the NCAA championship, made this comment:

> Once you start keeping score, winning's the bottom line. It's the American concept. If not, it's like playing your grandmother, and even then you try to win—unless she has a lot of money and you want to get some of it.

Pride in Your Accomplishments

When Joe Namath retired, he said the thing he was most proud of was "coming back from the adversity of those injuries. I never played as well as I would have liked to have played, but I played for 13 seasons when my doctor thought I would play for four. And I played despite a lot of adversity."

If you express genuine pride in your track record, the audience will sense your sincerity and share in your pride.

The Need to Practice

Prior to becoming a U.S. senator, Bill Bradley enjoyed an illustrious sports career—first as a basketball star at Princeton University, and later with the New York Knicks. When he was at Princeton, his father used to tell him, "Son, when you're not out practicing, someone else is. And when you meet that person, he's going to beat you."

Substitute Speaking

All is flux, nothing stays still.
Heracleitus

You're sitting in your office, the phone rings, and it's your boss, asking you to pinch-hit as a last-minute substitute speaker.

Of course you agree, since it feels more like a summons than an invitation. Then panic hits. What can you possibly say, especially when the audience has been looking forward to hearing someone else?

Relax. You're not the first person to be squeezed into a substitute speaking slot. These guidelines should help.

Acknowledge You're a Substitute

The audience already knows you're just filling in, so you might as well be gracious about it. Say you're pleased to step in and speak to them. If you have trouble expressing this sentiment without gagging, rehearse it a few times in the privacy of your bedroom. Keep repeating it until you really *do* feel pleased to be the substitute speaker.

Don't Apologize for the Speaker Who Canceled

Look at it this way: You aren't the person who canceled. You're the person who graciously stepped in! It's not your role to belabor someone else's cancelation.

Fortify yourself. Assume the blunt style of John Wayne:

"Never apologize and never explain—it's a sign of weakness."
Move forward with your own message.

Don't Gripe About the Short Notice

I once heard a grim-faced substitute complain, "I was just asked to give this speech when I came to work today, so I'm not really sure what to say." Need I remind you that this is hardly a way to warm up an audience? Lighten up—and stop griping.

Don't Worry About Being As Good As the Invited Speaker

Look at it this way: Would anyone in the audience be willing to trade places and stand in *your* shoes at the lectern? No way. They're all relieved *you're* the one who has to give the speech. So don't worry about meeting the audience's standards. Take Dale Carnegie's advice: "If you are speaking, forget everything but the subject. Never mind what others are thinking of you or your delivery. Just forget yourself and go ahead."

Speak from Your Own Perspective

You're under no obligation to second-guess the original speaker. In fact, you're under no obligation to stick to the same topic. If you don't like the assigned title, change it. It's *your* lectern now, so you can tell your own story and call your own shots.

Above All, Follow Franklin Delano Roosevelt's Advice

FDR once said, "Be sincere; be brief, be seated." Substitute speakers can find no better advice.

TOASTS

Never lose a chance of saying a kind word.
William Makepeace Thackeray

When President George Herbert Walker Bush made a historic visit to Poland in 1989, he ad-libbed a toast—urging that country's factions to "rise above the mistrust, to bring the Polish people together for a common purpose."

Then he asked General Jaruzelski to make a toast. Apparently, the general was caught off guard by the president's impromptu request. When Bush saw the surprised look on the general's face, he quickly grabbed the general's arm and said, "You don't have to do it." But the Polish leader came through, managing to ad-lib a toast that brought applause from the guests.

I suppose there are a couple of lessons in this story: You never know when you'll be asked to give a toast, and there never really is a gracious way out of it.

No matter how surprised—and unprepared—you might feel, the best thing to do is *gather your wits and give the toast.*

Please: no stammering, no apologies, no gee-I-never-thought-I'd-have-to-give-a-toast disclaimers. Just make the toast.

Of course, maybe you'll be lucky. Maybe they'll ask you ahead of time, so you can prepare a good toast. These suggestions should give you some ideas.

Graduation Toast

"You're leaving college now and going out into real life. And you have to realize that real life is not like college. Real life is like high school."

   Meryl Streep (speaking at Vassar College)

- *Give a nod to the graduate's hard work.* Did she take extra classes? Study in Europe? Pay for tuition by working every weekend? Now is the time to recognize this effort.

- *Note the graduate's drive to succeed.* Can you get a former teacher to provide a comment? Or ask a professor to share an example?

- *Cite the graduate's academic excellence.* Did he achieve high honors? Did she win special awards? Don't be shy. This is the time to salute excellence.

- *Include a personal story.* How have you seen the graduate change over the years? What admirable characteristics have remained the same?

- *Use an inspirational quotation.* "I toast you with the words of that famous suffragette, Lucy Stone, who changed women's lives with this philosophy: 'Make the world better.'"

Anniversary Toast

Throwing a party to salute 25 years of marriage? To celebrate the first year of a new business? To acknowledge 10 years of a successful partnership?

   Make a toast not just to the years themselves, but to the good things they represent.

   Keep it short. You don't have to recount everything that's occurred over the past 25 years. You're giving a toast . . . not a complete, documented history.

   Practice your toast several times before the event (so the words come out naturally). It's probably wise to have your toast written on a notecard in case a sudden case of the jitters turns your mind into jelly . . . but you should not (under any circumstances) look like you are reading the toast.

New-Baby Toast

- *Use an inspirational quotation.* Need a good source for inspirational lines? Check out a greeting card store. No kidding. Greeting cards are filled with short, touching, inspirational lines that can often double as terrific toasts.

- *Pay tribute to the parents.* And grandparents, too. "To the greatest grandparents in the world: May they live to be great grandparents!"

- *Make a toast to the child's health and happiness.*

Birthday Toast

- *Express affection and gratitude.* Journalist Murray Teigh Bloom offered this toast to his wife on her seventieth birthday: "Here's to Dellie, who's brought smiles or friendship or love to all of us here, and all of them to most of us."

- *Toast the person's health.*

- *Wish the person many more years of good times.* "May you live as long as you want, and never want as long as you live."

- *Use a light touch of humor.* "May you live to be a hundred—with an extra year added to repent."

- *When the person's age is a mystery:* "Here's to the most closely guarded secret in the whole country, your real age. No matter how old you are, you sure don't look it!"

Wedding Toast

- *Define marriage.* Drink to "a taste of paradise"—Shalom Aleichem; "the best method for getting acquainted"—Heywood

Broun; "an armed alliance against the outside world"—G.K. Chesterton.

- *Wish the bride and groom health, happiness, and prosperity.* Hard to go wrong with this triple blessing!

- *Wish them a smooth life.* A traditional toast to the bridal couple: "May all your troubles be little ones."

- *Wish all the celebrants much joy.* A toast straight from Shakespeare: "I drink to the general joy o' the whole table."

- *Toast both sets of parents.*

- *Consider a quote.* Remember how Walter Winchell described marriage: "Never above you. Never below you. Always beside you."

Some Cautions

Beware of last-minute jitters. A salesman once told me about the time he thought he'd "wing" a toast at his son's wedding. By the time he finally stood up to offer the wedding toast, he'd already had a few drinks. And out came "Here's to my son—and to his first wife." Ouch.

Pay attention to previous toasts, so you can respond accordingly. At the end of the Revolutionary War, Ben Franklin, as America's minister in Europe, attended a dinner in Paris with the British ambassador and the French foreign minister.

The British ambassador offered a toast "to George the Third, who, like the sun at noonday, spreads his light and illuminates the world." The French minister toasted "His Majesty, Louis the Sixteenth, who, like the moon, fills the earth with a soft, benevolent glow."

Franklin managed to top them both with this toast: "To George Washington, general of the armies of the United States, who, like Joshua of old, commanded both the sun and the moon to stand still, and both obeyed."

If you're worried about omitting someone, cover yourself by

including *everyone*. This old toast might do the trick: "Here's to the whole world, lest some damn fool take offense."

THE LOGISTICS

If You're Giving the Toast

1. Rise (if possible).

2. Speak with energy and sincerity. Your vocal personality will communicate at least as much as your words. Let your voice resonate with joy.

3. Bring your toast to a clear finish by using a formal indication: i.e., "Now, please join me in toasting————." (End with a firm, confident voice to indicate finality.)

4. Raise your glass to everyone (not just to the recipient). This body language will alert the whole audience—and they'll follow your lead.

5. Wrap up by saying "cheers!" (or any short line you'd like the guests to repeat).

6. Clink the recipient's glass . . . or "air clink." (This will signal the entire room to do the same.)

7. Sip . . . and everyone else will sip with you.

8. Smile at the recipient.

9. Smile at the whole room.

Don't worry about forgetting any of these steps. If you speak from the heart and toast with sincerity, you'll do fine.

If You're the Recipient of the Toast

1. Sit (if possible).

2. There's no need for you to raise your glass before the toast.

3. Just listen to the toaster and enjoy the moment. It doesn't happen every day!

4. After you've received the toast? Smile . . . thank the toaster . . . perhaps raise your glass in appreciation to the entire room . . . or gesture openly to express your gratitude to the group.

5. Let the toaster sip first . . . then take your sip.

6. Stay "in the moment." No nervous fidgeting, please.

WORDS OF WELCOME

Welcome is the best dish in the kitchen.
Old Scottish saying

Want to greet new staff members? Say hello to a fresh group of volunteers? Welcome the freshman class to your school?

Offer a few words of welcome that will:

- make them feel at home
- recognize their special talents
- respect their various backgrounds
- get them in the right mood
- tell them about your organization
- let them know what's ahead.

Here are some ideas that have worked for others:

Encourage New Members to Plunge Right In

When Joan Konner, dean of Columbia University Graduate School of Journalism, delivered opening day remarks, she said:

> Everything you do, everyone you meet, every book you read, every event you attend will tell you a story, and possibly a truth. . . .
>
> So keep your eyes open. Then let your mind go to work on what you see. Out will pop a reality of your own making.

If you report it accurately and responsibly, you'll be a fine reporter.

If you discern the pattern underlying it, you are a scientist.

And if you can make others see something new, or something old in a new way, you're an artist, discovering a reality and shaping it, as well.

The best reporters are all of these.

And now it's time to get out of the taxi and to go out into the field. You've got the background. It's time to find the story.

Build a Theme Around the Motto of Your Organization

Does your school, group, or business have an official motto? You can build a theme around that slogan.

Cite Your Goals for the Coming Year

Do you plan to open x new stores? Increase test scores by x percent? Build a better image in the community? Now's the time to share your goals with the people who will help achieve them.

Take Action

Find specific ways to involve each new participant. Let everyone feel they're part of the team right from the beginning. Above all, let them see that your "words of welcome" are more than mere words. Back up your good intentions with good actions:

- Assign mentors.
- Offer projects.
- Plan progress checks.
- Schedule regular feedback sessions.

- Encourage new ideas.
- Provide a "suggestion box."
- Cite their achievements for all to see.

Encourage a Sense of Teamwork

When you welcome your new members on board, make them feel part of the team right from the start. Talk about the standards of your group, so they know what's expected of them. Also talk about the resources of your group, so they know where they can turn for extra support.

Share Your Enthusiasm

Cite the sage advice of Henry David Thoreau: "Do what you love." And then encourage the entire group to do exactly that.

Let your own enthusiasm shine through. Words of welcome mean more when they're spoken with openness, energy, and sincerity.

Find Some Humor in the Situation

At the Washington swearing-in ceremony of U.S. Attorney General Nicholas Katzenbach and Deputy Attorney General Ramsey Clark, President Lyndon Johnson welcomed the two on board with this quip: "A town that can't support one lawyer can always support two." Hard to argue with that.

RESOURCES

APPENDIX

PREPARATION CHECKLIST: NINE STEPS TO A BETTER SPEECH

_____ 1. *Focus your topic.* You can't say everything. Choose wisely.

_____ 2. *Analyze your audience.* What do they want to hear about your topic? What do they need to know?

_____ 3. *Target the most interesting research.* Omit tedious details. Avoid information overload. Remember this bit of wisdom from advertising genius David Ogilvy: "Nobody ever sold anybody anything by boring them to death."

_____ 4. *Organize your material.* You need a beginning, a middle, and an ending. Tell them what you're going to tell them . . . tell them . . . and then tell them what you told them.

_____ 5. *Simplify your language.* Make your presentation easy to understand.

_____ 6. *Use rhetorical devices to create style.* (See the Glossary for ideas.)

_____ 7. *Use humor; don't abuse humor.* You'll never get the chance to undo a tasteless joke. When in doubt, leave it out.

_____ 8. *Allow enough rehearsal time to improve delivery.* Get better each time you practice.

_____ 9. *Consider getting media coverage.* Special occasion speeches often deserve media attention. Think about your publicity options.

(Source: *www.joandetz.com*)

GLOSSARY OF
RHETORICAL TECHNIQUES

Alliteration: Repeating the same sound at the beginning of two or more consecutive words (or words in close proximity). "Drinking plus driving spell death and disaster." (President Ronald Reagan)

Anecdote: A brief narrative that tells about an interesting (and possibly amusing) incident . . . in other words, a true story designed to engage the audience.

Colloquial Language: A relaxed, conversational, informal speaking style. "You can put wings on a pig, but you don't make it an eagle." (President William Clinton)

Ellipsis: Leaving out words to establish a stronger cadence. Use three dots (. . .) to indicate an ellipsis.

Hyperbole: Exaggeration used to drive home a point. When asked about the chances of a particular bill passing the Senate, Republican Minority Leader Everett Dirksen strung out his response for full effect: "Ha, ha, ha. And, I might add, ho, ho, ho."

Imagery: Figurative language; ornamental speech designed to create a vivid picture in the audience's mind.
- Winston Churchill: the iron curtain
- President Theodore Roosevelt: the big stick

Parallel Structure: Placing words or phrases in similar patterns. Parallel structure provides a sense of balance for the listener and creates an emotional appeal. "The wealthy grow ever wealthier, while the poor grow ever poorer." (Pope John Paul II, in Cuba)

Repetition: Repeating words, phrases, or whole sentences for stylistic effect.

Rhetorical Question: A question not intended to elicit an answer, but inserted into the speech for stylistic effect. Samples:
- Why should we do this?
- Who cares?
- Where do we go next?

Simile. A figure of speech comparing one thing or action to something of a different kind or quality. "[Dealing with bureaucracy] is like trying to nail jelly to the wall." (President John F. Kennedy)

Triad: A rhetorical grouping of three items (words, phrases, sentences). President George W. Bush, in his address to the nation on September 20, 2001, used this triad in response to the 9/11 tragedy: "We will not tire . . . we will not falter . . . we will not fail."

Word play: Creatively positioning words to make a compelling (and often amusing) point. "Numerous politicians have seized absolute power and muzzled the press. Never in history has the press seized absolute power and muzzled the politicians." (TV newsman David Brinkley)

ANNOTATED BIBLIOGRAPHY

WHERE TO FIND GREAT QUOTES AND ANECDOTES

BOOKS

America

Barnett, Alex. *The Quotable American*. (Guilford, CT: Lyons Press, 2002.) Excellent material for patriotic celebrations, military ceremonies, commencements, and national observances. Chapters include:

- Defining Moments
- Sea to Shining Sea—The American Landscape
- Democracy
- The Melting Pot
- War
- The Arts in America
- The Sporting Life

Reagan, Michael. *In the Words of Ronald Reagan*. (Nashville, TN: Nelson Books, 2004.) The wit, wisdom, and eternal optimism of America's 40th president.

Anecdotes

Bernard, Andre, and Clifton Fadiman. *Barlett's Book of Anecdotes*. Revised edition. (Boston: Little Brown, 2001.) This remains the best all-around source for anecdotes. Topics are wide-ranging:

- Bismarck receiving the Iron Cross award.

- Architect Addison Mizner sharing his philosophy of "construction first, blueprints afterward."
- Sojourner Truth testing the streetcar antidiscrimination law in Washington, D.C.

Well-researched and well-documented—with a detailed subject index, source list, and bibliography.

Anniversaries

Dickson, Paul. *Timelines: Day by Day and Trend by Trend*. (Reading, MA: Addison Wesley Publishing, 1991.) Celebrating the anniversary of your organization? Turn to this book first. You'll get great glimpses into each year from 1945 to the present. For example, in 1967:

- The first home microwave was introduced by Amana—becoming both a noun and a verb.
- The world's first successful heart transplant operation was performed in Capetown, South Africa, by Dr. Christiaan Barnard.

Banquets and Celebratory Meals

Cader, Michael, with Debby Roth. *Eat These Words*. (New York: Harper-Collins, 1991.) Speaking at a United Way fund-raising breakfast? Hosting a mother-daughter tea? Running an awards dinner? You might find some entertaining lines in this little book.

Egerton, March, ed. *Since Eve Ate Apples*. (Portland, OR: Tsunami Press, 1994.) This is an outstanding reference book—well researched and well organized. Includes a wide range of sources:

- "An army marches on its stomach." (Napoleon Bonaparte)
- "A hungry man is not a free man." (Adlai Stevenson)
- "I refuse to spend my life worrying about what I eat. There is no pleasure worth foregoing just for an extra three years in the geriatric ward." (John Mortimer)

I particularly like this entry from President Jimmy Carter's White House diary: ". . . when Rosalynn was visiting the White House, some of our staff asked the cooks if they thought that they could prepare the kind of meals which we enjoyed in the South, and the cook said, 'Yes, Ma'am, we've been fixing that kind of food for the servants for a long time!'"

Robbins, Maria Polushkined. *The Cook's Quotation Book*. (New York: Penguin Books, 1984.) You'll find lines to use in a wide variety of speeches:

- "Omlettes are not made without breaking eggs." (Robespierre)
- "I do not think that anything serious should be done after dinner, as nothing should be before breakfast." (George Santsbury)

This line would add life to any wedding anniversary toast: "My wife and I tried to breakfast together, but we had to stop or our marriage would have been wrecked." (Winston Churchill)

Birthday Celebrations

Lewman, David. *When I Was Your Age: Remarkable Achievements of Writers, Artists, and Musicians at Every Age from 1 to 100*. (Chicago: Triumph Books, 1997.)

- At age fifty-five, Mark Twain learns to ride a bicycle.
- At age seventy-six, Grandma Moses gives up embroidery and begins to paint.

Morris, Desmond. *The Book of Ages*. (New York: Penguin, 1983.) There are newer books—but none better if you want to add some life to a birthday toast. Consider:

- Dante's definition of 25 as "the end of childhood."
- Sophie Tucker's famous song, "Life Begins at 40."
- Bob Hope's definition of "middle age": "You know you're middle aged when your age starts to show around your middle."

Sampson, Anthony and Sally. *The Oxford Book of Ages*. (New York: Oxford University Press, 1988.) Quotations and poetry about every year of life—from one to one hundred.

- "At twenty years of age, the will reigns; at thirty, the wit; and at forty, the judgment." (Benjamin Franklin)
- "The first forty years of life furnish the text, while the remaining thirty supply the commentary." (Schopenhauer)

- "My life's span has reached seventy,
  If I don't enjoy myself now, when shall I?"
  (The Rubaiyat of Omar Khayyam)

Celebrations

Frank, Catherine. *Quotations for All Occasions.* (New York: Columbia University Press, 2000.) This book earns my highest praise. You will find well-documented material for an extraordinarily wide range of occasions, including:

- Chinese New Year
- Valentine's Day
- February 29
- St. Patrick's Day
- April Fool's Day
- Ramadan
- Mother's Day
- Memorial Day
- Rosh Hashanah
- Christmas
- Kwanzaa

You'll also find material for lifestyle celebrations:

- first baby
- turning 16
- quitting smoking
- apology
- becoming a grandparent

Former First Lady Betty Ford on "Recovery": "Sometimes, I'm almost sorry for people who *haven't* been alcoholic, because I know things that a person who's never been sick doesn't know. I had to climb over hurdles. I had to experience the disease, be sick with it, and then experience recovery."

Author and Holocaust survivor Elie Wiesel on "Fridays": "I shall never forget Shabbat in my town. When I shall have forgotten everything else, my memory will still retain the atmosphere of holiday, of serenity pervading even the poorest houses: the white tablecloths, the candles, the meticulously combed little girls, the men on their way to the synagogue. When my town shall fade into the abyss of time, I will continue to remember the light and the warmth it radiated on Shabbat."

Clergy

Jones, Loyal. *The Preacher Joke Book: Religious Anecdotes from the Oral Tradition*. (Little Rock, AR: August House Publishers, 1989.) Is your minister retiring? Or celebrating a major anniversary? Turn here to find funny stories. My favorite: the radio preacher who announced, "Do you want to learn what hell is? Tune in next week. We'll be featuring our organist."

Commencements

Ross, Alan, ed. *Speaking of Graduation*. (Nashville, TN: Walnut Grove Press, 2001.) Excerpts from a wide range of graduation speeches.

Daily Listings

Mason, Eileen. *Witty Words*. (New York: Sterling Publishing, 1992.) Find clever quotes related on the day of your speech.

- March 14 (the birthday of physicist Albert Einstein): "When you sit with a nice girl for two hours, you think it's only a minute. But when you sit on a hot stove for a minute, you think it's two hours. That's relativity."
- November 9: Check the Batteries in Your Flashlight Day
- December 17: Wright Brothers Day

Environment

Rodes, Barbara K., and Odell Rice. *A Dictionary of Environmental Quotations*. (Baltimore: The Johns Hopkins University Press, 1992.) Giving an Earth Day speech? Or dedicating a new recycling center? This book will give you excellent quotations about the environment.

Fripp, Jon, Michael, and Deborah. *Speaking of Science: Notable Quotes on Science, Engineering, and the Environment.* (Eagle Rock, VA: LLH Technology Publishing, 2000.) A collection of pithy quotes.

- Benjamin Franklin: "When the well's dry, we know the worth of water."
- Ralph Waldo Emerson: "What is a weed? A plant whose virtues have not yet been discovered."

Ethnic

Hanki, Joseph. *Arabic Proverbs.* (New York: Hippocrene Books, 1998). This bilingual proverb collection contains 600 Arabic proverbs with side-by-side English translations (and equivalent English proverbs where appropriate).

De Ley, Gerd. *African Proverbs.* (New York: Hippocrene Books, 1999.) An extensive collection of 1,755 proverbs spans all regions of the African continent. Each proverb is arranged alphabetically by key word and includes the country, province, or tribe of origin. Includes bibliography and information glossary.

Sherman, Josepha. *A Sampler of Jewish American Folklore.* (Little Rock, AR: August House Publishers, 1992.) Chapters cover:

- life and celebrations
- love and marriage
- birth and childhood
- death and mourning
- clever folk and survivors
- allegories and moral tales
- humorous tales
- proverbs and riddles

Bibliography—plus an extraordinarily detailed notes section, where you can learn more about sources.

West, John O. *Mexican-American Folklore.* (Little Rock, AK: August House Publishers, 1988.) Legends, songs, festivals, tales of saints, proverbs.

Eulogies

McNees, Pat, ed. *Dying: A Book of Comfort*. (New York: Warner Books, 1998.) A valuable resource for anyone who must give a eulogy. A diverse and inspirational cross-section of sources: from Mark Twain to Emily Dickinson, from Anne Morrow Lindberg to *The Tibetan Book of Living and Dying*. Many selections are suitable for reading at funerals and memorial services. Special sections focus on the death of a parent, the death of a child, a death by suicide, and violent or sudden deaths. Very well organized. Indexed by names, titles, and selected first lines.

History

Axelrod, Alan. *The Quotable Historian*. (New York: McGraw-Hill, 2000.) You'll find sections on a wide range of themes.

Humor

Perret, Gene and Linda, *Funny Business*. (Englewood Cliffs, NJ: Prentice-Hall, 1990.) Looking for a clever one-liner about some aspect of business life? Start here. This book is very well organized—and chock-full of useable material. You'll find quips for a wide range of office topics:

- management vs. labor
- résumés
- the job interview
- mandatory retirement
- telephone etiquette
- commuting to work
- relocation
- expense accounts

Plus an entire section is devoted to "occupations we all deal with." You'll find one-liners to toast or roast:

- accountants
- bankers
- consultants
- doctors

- lawyers
- nurses
- salespeople

Law

Shrager, David, and Elizabeth Frost. *The Quotable Lawyer.* (New York: Facts on File, 1986.) Well-researched quotes on every aspect of the law:

- contracts: "To break an oral agreement which is not legally binding is morally wrong." (Talmud)
- guilt: ". . . the two-fold aim [of criminal justice] is that guilt should not escape or innocence suffer." (Berger v. United States)
- the press: "People everywhere confuse what they read in the newspapers with news." (A. J. Liebling)

Excellent research: bibliography, subject index, author index.

Martin Luther King Jr. Day

King, Coretta Scott, selected by. *The Words of Martin Luther King Jr.* (New York: Newmarket Press, 1987.) These selections from MLK's speeches and writings share Dr. King's thoughts on seven major themes:

- the community of man
- racism
- civil rights
- justice and freedom
- faith and religion
- nonviolence
- peace

Coretta Scott King's introduction offers a powerful and eloquent tribute to her husband. The book features the full text of President Ronald Reagan's proclamation marking the first observance of Dr. Martin Luther King's birthday as a national holiday. Provides a detailed chronology of events.

World Almanac Editors. *Words That Set Us Free*, (New York: World Almanac, 1992.) This book provides a "chronology of America's struggle for equal justice and civil rights." You'll find excerpts from the laws, speeches, documents, and essays that changed the conscience of the nation. Bibliography and index. Sources include:

- Abigail Adams
- Frederick Douglass
- Lucy Stone
- W.E.B. Dubois
- Hubert Humphrey
- Shirley Chisholm
- Jesse Jackson

Men

Allen, Jessica. *Quotable Men of the Twentieth Century.* (New York: William Morrow and Company, 1999.) Wide range of topics:

- athletes: "I'm throwing twice as hard as I ever did. The ball's just not going as fast." (Lefty Gomez)
- gender gap: "Women who seek to be equal with men lack ambition." (Timothy Leary)
- race: "I realize that I'm black, but I like to be viewed as a person, and that's everybody's wish." (Michael Jordan)
- women: "My advice to the women's clubs of America is to raise more hell and fewer dahlias." (William Allen White)
- cats: "Cats are intended to teach us that not everything in nature has a function." (Garrison Keillor)
- success: "Behind every successful man stands a surprised mother-in-law." (Hubert Humphrey)

Military

Charlton, James, ed. *The Military Quotation Book.* (New York: St. Martin's Press, 1990.) Observations about war, courage, patriotism, combat, victory, and defeat. More than 600 quotations spanning 4,000 years of war and peace.

- "War is the unfolding of miscalculations." (Barbara Tuchman)

- "It is enough for the world to know that I am a soldier." (Gen. William Sherman)
- "I have given instructions that I be informed every time one of our soldiers is killed, even if it is in the middle of the night. When President Nasser leaves instructions that he is to be awakened in the middle of the night if an Egyptian solider is killed, there will be peace." (Golda Meir)

Politics

Tomlinson, Gerald. *Speaker's Treasury of Political Stories, Anecdotes & Humor.* (Englewood Cliffs, NJ: Prentice-Hall, 1990.) A cross-section of material:

- Benjamin Franklin's reputation for stinginess
- Daniel Webster's response to criticism: "I make it a point never to shovel out the path until the snow is done falling."
- Ron Ziegler (press secretary to President Richard Nixon) revising the White House version of the Watergate story . . . and dismissing earlier versions as "inoperative statements"

Note: This book also contains a very helpful "calendar of political events"—listing famous moments in politics for each day of the year. Index, and an excellent bibliography.

Udall, Morris K. *Too Funny to Be President.* (New York: Henry Holt and Company, 1988.) Mo Udall was once named the most respected and most effective member of U.S. Congress. In this book, you'll find a mother lode of political stories, jokes, and anecdotes—seldom seen elsewhere. A few favorites . . .

- The famed mayor of New York City, Jimmy Walker, who was known for being quick-witted, was once asked by then governor of New York Franklin Delano Roosevelt, "Why is it that the Irish always answer a question with a question?"

   "Do we now?" responded Hizzoner.
- A guest seated in the visitors' gallery of the Senate watched intently as the chaplain opened the day's proceedings with an invocation. "Does the chaplain pray for the senators?" he asked.

"No," replied his companion, "he looks at the senators and then prays for the country."

- Barry Goldwater's father was Jewish, but he married a gentile, and Barry himself was raised as an Episcopalian. During the early stages of the 1964 presidential campaign, when it looked as if Barry might defeat Lyndon Johnson, the journalist Harry Golden quipped, "Somehow I always knew that our first Jewish president would be an Episcopalian."
- Speaking of taxes, Adlai Stevenson said: "There was a time when a fool and his money were soon parted; now it happens to everybody."

Whitman, William B. *The Quotable Politician.* (Guildford, CT: Lyons Press, 2003.) The author was formerly a diplomat with the U.S. foreign service, and his international experience contributes to the value of this book. It offers hard-to-find comments from a wide range of international leaders (from Margaret Thatcher to Boris Yeltsin to Zhou Enlai), in addition to quotes from U.S. politicians.

- "The illegal we do immediately. The unconstitutional takes a little longer." (Henry Kissinger)

Presidents

Boller Paul. F. Jr. *Presidential Anecdotes.* Revised edition. (New York: Oxford University Press, 1996.) Detailed anecdotes covering everything from military strategy to legislation.

Frost, Elizabeth. *The Bully Pulpit.* (New York: Facts on File, 1988.) This is your single best source for presidential quotes. Very well researched and documented.

Retirements

Pasta, Elmer. *Compete Book of Roasts, Toasts, and Boasts* by Elmer Pasta. (West Nyack, NY: Parker Publishing, 1982.) This book has been on my bookshelf for decades—and it will always remain a useful reference book because its entries are timeless. It covers every conceivable occupation: from bookkeepers to beekeepers . . . from X-ray technicians to lifeguards.

Roasts

Evans III, William R., and Andrew Frothingham. *Well-Done Roasts*. (New York: St. Martin's Press, 1992.) Topics included are:

- dentists: "To the man who deals with the tooth, the whole tooth, and nothing but the tooth."
- clergy: "To our minister—who would rather preach than practice."
- Washington, D.C.: "Our country's capital, where the roads, and everything else, go around in circles."
- tennis: "Here's to tennis—may we all have net gains."

Toasts

Conover, Jennifer Rahel. *Toasts for Every Occasion*. (New York: New American Library, 2001.) Need to say a few words at your daughter's birthday . . . your boss's baby shower . . . your brother's wedding? You'll find 1,300 lively toasts in this book, from the likes of W. C. Fields, Humphrey Bogart, Mae West, Walter Winchell, and Gloria Steinem.

Evans III, William R., and Andrew Frothingham. *Crisp Toasts*. (New York: St. Martin's Press, 1992.) Clever lines for many categories, including:

- absent friends
- courage
- husbands and wives
- parents
- peace

Note: This book also offers toasts for various professions, including:

- architects
- bankers
- clergy
- dentists
- lawyers
- stockbrokers

Women

Partnow, Elaine. *The Quotable Woman: From 1800 to 1981.* (New York: Facts on File, 1982.) The first major collection of quotations by women—and still the most definitive. An outstanding reference work. Biographical index, subject index.

- Rachel Carson: "In an age when man has forgotten his origins and is blind even to his most essential needs for survival, water . . . has become the victim of his indifference."
- Agatha Christie: "One doesn't recognize in one's life the really important moments—not until it's too late."
- Harriet Tubman: "I had reasoned this out in my mind, there was two things I had a right to, liberty and death. If I could not have one, I would have the other, for no man should take me alive."

Partnow, Elaine. *The Quotable Woman: From Eve to 1799.* (New York: Facts on File, 1986.) Excellent opening section of quotations from the Bible. Note: This volume also offers a particularly strong selection of international quotations: Japanese writers . . . Polish poets . . . Spanish philosophers . . . Iranian poets . . . Italian diplomats.

WEB SITES

Anecdotes

www.bizmove.com Assorted anecdotes (both humorous and inspirational).

www.idea-bank.com A reliable pay site.

www.storybin.com Stories, parables, and writings with a "positive-thinking" approach.

Nostalgia/Trivia

www.1960sflashback.com Covers tidbits from sports, news, TV, and books.

www.80snostalgia.com Offers interesting "on this day" items for both the eighties and the seventies.

Proverbs

www.aphorismsgalore.com Quirky entries in wide-ranging categories.

www.good-english.com Give a key word, and find the expression you need.

Research Sites

www.bibliomania.com Texts, study guides, and resources (explore the King James Bible, the Koran, etc).

www.infoplease.com Giving a speech on June 3? Find historical items related to this date in history.

www.lii.org This librarians' index to the Internet sets the standard.

www.naturalscience.com Quick access to articles, news, and books.

www.refdesk.com An excellent resource since 1995. Many links to other useful sites.

Quotations

www.bartleby.com Offers *Simpson's Contemporary Quotations, Bartlett's Book of Familiar Quotations, Columbia World of Quotations* . . . and much more.

www.bemorecreative.com Search fifty thousand quotations (and biographical information) from more than three thousand famous sources.

www.brainyquote.com Search topics from age to work. Search sources by job category: from actress and astronaut to theologian and vice president.

Sermons

www.sermoncentral.com Wide-ranging sermon topics: addiction, children, holidays, poverty.

Speeches

www.pbs.org Runs the gamut from Mark Twain's seventieth birthday speech to Senator John Kerry's acceptance speech.

www.historychannel.com Texts of speeches by business executives, politicians, and academics.

www.historyplace.com Features a "speech of the week." Offers an eclectic assortment of speech manuscripts.

www.dtic.mil.com The tagline proclaims, "Making Government User-Friendly" . . . and its easy-to-use format delivers on that promise.

www.school-for-champions.com A great resource for presidential inaugural addresses.

www.vital-speeches.com Speeches on current events in government, education, business, culture, and the economy.

Toasts

www.stpatricksday.com Irish toasts galore.

INDEX OF SPEAKERS